"In a time of unprecedented challenges, we are all facing 'giants' on many fronts. Ed Norwood has written a book that will help people of faith (and those searching for faith) to be victorious against the giants they face. This book takes on seven of the biggest giants anyone can face and uses timeless truth to teach how to defeat them. You will learn from his example and instruction and benefit from his encouragement and inspiration."

—*Mark Sanborn, NYT and WSJ bestselling author of* The Fred Factor
President, Sanborn & Associates, Inc.

"Powerful and impactful! Ed is an incredible man and friend with a very unique personal story. His passion is contagious! He identifies God's dreams for His children and the giants in the way of fulfilling these dreams. This is a must-read for anyone excited to use biblical weapons to help defeat these giants in life and chase their dreams! Get reading and let's go!"

—*Bruce Tollner, Co-Author of* Sidelined *with Indianapolis Colts Coach Chuck Pagano/NFL Agent/ Owner Rep 1 which represents Jared Goff, Carson Wentz, Marcus Mariota, Ben Roethlisberger and many others.*

"In *Be A Giant Killer*, Ed Norwood equips the reader to be able to readily identify the enemies that hinder us, and then conquer them. Defining the problem well is half the battle. This is gold to those who are ready to be victorious warriors."

—*Bishop Dale C. Bronner, D. Min.*
Founder/Senior Pastor
Word of Faith Family Worship Cathedral

Atlanta, GA "The terrible reality is that in this great world, in this great God's world, there are evils. These evils aren't the apocalyptic wars and pestilence and such. These evils attack one's soul, one's being. Think of rage, abuse, and mental ill-health. These evils surround each of us and want to limit us; lower us; lessen us. If you, or someone you love, is struggling, fighting these evils please read Ed Norwood's fabulous, faith-based *Be A Giant Killer: Overcoming Your Everyday Goliaths*. Become a 'giant killer' to kill evils and conquer these demons to delight in your God-given fulfilling life."

—*Jeffrey J. Fox is a New York Times Best Selling author of thirteen books including* How to Become CEO *and* How to Be a Great Boss, *which have been published in over 35 languages.*

"Home Run, I highly recommend *Be A Giant Killer*. Ed knows from first-hand experience that it's possible to overcome and exceed no matter the circumstance."

—Maina Mwaura, Public speaker, Journalist, and Consultant (conducting over 300 interviews with Christian Influencers, e.g. Promise Keepers, Barna, and Christian Headlines)

"While many books have been written on *facing giants, Be A Giant Killer* by Ed Norwood provides unique insights by paralleling the giants the Israelites faced as they approached the Promised Land, led by Joshua, with the giants we all face at one time or another. Drawing extensively on Scripture, the author applies biblical insights to overcoming the giants we face daily—and achieving our God-given dreams. On top of vivid personal illustrations, the author introduces his family's loss in The People's Temple cult and how a 'giant' got away with murdering 913 people in the jungles of Jonestown (Guyana) because Jim Jones was not stopped. There are enough encouragements and warnings to last a lifetime."

—Les Stobbe, Writer Coach

BE A
GIANT
KILLER

Overcoming Your Everyday Goliaths

ED NORWOOD

FREILING PUBLISHING

Published by Freiling Publishing,
a division of Freiling Agency, LLC.

P.O. Box 1264,
Warrenton, VA 20188

www.FreilingPublishing.com

ISBN: 978-1-950948-92-5

Printed in the United States of America

DEDICATION

This book is dedicated to:

My beautiful wife Anu, my amazing three children,
Jasmine, Joshua, and Josiah who, together,
inspire me to be more.

MISSION:

To restore family history by effectively producing
giant killers that influence the next generation.
The next chapters belong to you.

#IAMAGIANTKILLER

TABLE OF CONTENTS

Prologue   I Am a Giant Killer.............................xi

Chapter 1   Tackling Our Goliath 17

Chapter 2   The Seven Giants Present........................... 33

Chapter 3   The Giant of Fear (The Hittite)................... 43

Chapter 4   The Giant of Dissatisfaction
                (The Girgashite).. 61

Chapter 5   The Giant of Unforgiveness
                (The Amorite) 83

Chapter 6   The Giant of Addiction
                (The Canaanite) 103

Chapter 7   The Giant of Laziness (The Perizzite) 127

Chapter 8   The Giant of Procrastination
                (The Hivite) 151

Chapter 9   The Giant of Folly (The Jebusite)............. 167

Chapter 10   Our Family History.................................. 185

Chapter 11   A Critical Spirit 211

Chapter 12   Contaminated Dreams 225

Chapter 13   The Wilderness....................................... 251

Chapter 14   An Unconventional Generation................. 277

Epilogue   Final Word.. 287

References 293

PROLOGUE

I AM A GIANT KILLER

At only 5'10", Jim Jones was a murderous giant. He intimidated, manipulated, lied to, terrorized, and killed his followers in one of the largest single-loss U.S. civilian events in American history. On November 18, 1978, Jim Jones massacred 918 people in Jonestown, Guyana, leaving behind a disturbing scene of bloated bodies and mounds of decaying corpses, rotting in the unrelenting tropical heat of the jungle sun.

"I can't sleep," said one of the first responders. "I cannot get the small children out of my mind." Hundreds of innocent children littered the compound, their tiny bodies poisoned and destroyed by the absolute evil of Jim Jones.

One of those children could have been me. In total, twenty-seven of my family members were slaughtered at Jonestown. According to my late great-grandmother, who stayed in America, seventeen of these family members were children.

These haunting images of Jonestown and the unforgettable stench of overwhelming decay tormented U.S.

military recovery workers, who later reported the number of children they saw that day was the most disturbing thing they encountered. Found in the pavilion of the camp were vats of cyanide-laced Flavor Aid that Jones ordered his followers to drink at gunpoint or face immediate execution. The expression "Don't drink the Kool-Aid" was coined following the gruesome discovery of this mass murder scene as Jones instructed the children to be eliminated first, stripping the adults of hope or a will to fight and survive.

Jones had just committed a federal offense by assassinating an elected member of the U.S. Congress, California Congressman Leo Ryan. Therefore, taking the lives of so many others meant little to him.

George Corey, an attorney and friend of Congressman Ryan, once said this about him: "He [Ryan] would march into the heart of hell to see it firsthand." When Ryan's friend of over 25 years, Sammy Houston, alleged that his two grandchildren were held in a dense South American jungle, surrounded by poisonous snakes and against their (and his daughter's) will by cult leader Jim Jones, Ryan promised to do all in his power to get them out.

Congressman Ryan was a known maverick and fact-finder who sought the truth at any cost. Following the Watts riots in 1965, which resulted in thirty-four deaths, Ryan lived with an African American family and worked in the community as a substitute teacher to understand the conditions that led to such discontentment. Once, while chairing a committee investigating prison reform, he anonymously had himself admitted as an inmate to Folsom Prison for ten days. Another time, on a fact-finding mission to Newfoundland, he lay on ice between fur hunters and baby harp seals.

Ryan arrived in Guyana on November 14, 1978, to investigate human rights violations alleged by concerned relatives, refugees, and his good friend Sam. Four days later, he was shot at point-blank range on the Port Kaituma airstrip, trying to take defectors home from a dangerous settlement called Jonestown, Guyana.

It was his last act of heroism.

Later that night, on November 18, 1978, Jim Jones would order the deaths of all the members of his cult. Dissidents of the People's Temple reported to the FBI that Jim Jones had developed incredible control over his people: he regularly administered tests of their loyalty by having them drink a liquid purported to be poison. In the event they tried to leave, he had them sign numerous confessions of incest, child abuse, and other crimes as well, including statements of intent to kill the President and Vice President of the United States.

Jones frequently threatened violence and kidnapping if he were to be captured, and he had assassination teams against public officials in place to retaliate. Temple dissidents were on a hit list if they defected. My mom and I were on that list. Although not members, my mother began to tell my family (the first African American members of People's Temple) of the repeated dreams she had of Jones kidnapping my cousins and killing them in a jungle. As a result, Jones wanted her dead. So, she hid me in Daly City, California, for several years to spare my life.

Several of my close cousins weren't so fortunate.

Upon returning home from Petrini's Supermarket in San Francisco one day, my uncle came home to find his home ransacked and his wife and seven children, Doris, Karen, Barry, Lisa, Freddie Jr., Adrienne, Cassandra, and Alicia, gone.

They never came home.

My uncle's heart was hardened to God for the rest of his life (until on his death bed) because of the tragic loss of his family in Jonestown. He never recovered.

Too often, we marginalize past traumas, losses, or regrets.

We say things like:

"I'm fine."

"Well, that was then; this is now."

"It is what it is."

"Whatever doesn't kill you makes you stronger. "

"I didn't need them, anyhow."

Then why does it still hurt?

Why do we still get angry when triggered or reminded of it?

The unspoken pain or the little boy or girl in us deserves to be heard.

What we do today matters. It affects those after us. We either inspire or misfire the next generation, impress or confess our sins to them, steal or help fulfill the dreams in their heart. We have a choice. We can cower or act with courage. We can fight our giants or fall victim to them. Jim Jones was a Goliath. But I serve a God who raises generational giant killers in families and industries. I am a giant killer. Through my story, you can learn how to be a giant killer too.

#IAmAGiantKiller

CHAPTER 1

TACKLING OUR GOLIATH

Since the beginning of time, there have been giants.

Giants are big—they are tyrants. They represent a person or thing marked by exceptionally great size, magnitude, extraordinary power, significance, or importance. Giants exist to intimidate you to inaction. To not finish what you started. Not follow up. Not fight for your destiny. Not protest your rights to improve life skills or prevent future injury. Not sharpen your weapons or be great.

There are giants of all kinds—doubt, fear, addictions, diseases, family history, troublesome people, and poverty. Even governments and corporations can be Goliaths. And yes, some so-called churches or leaders (*e.g.*, Jim Jones) can be giants opposing you. You can be your own giant standing in the way of your dreams.

The Bible is a book of family history, good and bad, of how men and women had to overcome giants to achieve their destiny. We find the earliest giants mentioned by name in Genesis 6:4-8:

In those days, and for some time after, giant Nephilites lived on the earth, for whenever the sons of God had intercourse with women, they gave birth to children who became the heroes and famous warriors of ancient times. The LORD observed the extent of human wickedness on the earth, and he saw that everything they thought or imagined was consistently and totally evil. So the LORD was sorry he had ever made them and put them on the earth. It broke his heart. And the LORD said, "I will wipe this human race I have created from the face of the earth. Yes, and I will destroy every living thing—all the people, the large animals, the small animals that scurry along the ground, and even the birds of the sky. I am sorry I ever made them." But Noah found favor with the LORD. (NLT, emphasis added)

In a generation where the wickedness of men and women was great—where every imagination, thought, and intention was evil—Noah found grace in the eyes of God. In his day, God used a flood to drown the voice of giants on the earth. Today, God uses giant killers. You and I must silence the voice of our Goliath.

Many of us this year are facing or reviving new giants— giants we never imagined would creep into our lives.

Be A Giant Killer is a book on how family history (and bad habits) can affect everything we do in life. It is a giant we must not run from, but toward—to transform the experience we had as children, before it is transmitted to the next generation.

Giants exist to intimidate us. To make us conclude from evil reports:

- "No one survives this kind of cancer. I'll die with this diagnosis."
- "No marriage has ever succeeded in my family. I'll end up divorced."
- "No one has ever obtained their college degree. I'll be a dropout too."
- "I'll never amount to anything. My life is worthless."
- "Our family has always lived in poverty. I'll be on welfare too."

What is the Goliath facing your life, purpose, dream, and God-given ability? Maybe it is a problem you can't fix. A marriage on the brink of divorce. A legal battle. A betrayal by someone you love. A hidden secret. A shameful past. A fear depriving you from living out your God-ordained calling.

We all have them. For every unfulfilled dream, there is a giant dispatched to try and rob you of it.

And yet the Bible has plenty to say about facing giants. Probably the most prominent story is that of David and Goliath. We find the story in 1 Samuel 17:8-11:

Goliath stood and shouted a taunt across to the Israelites. 'Why are you all coming out to fight?' he called. 'I am the Philistine champion, but you are only the servants of Saul. Choose one man to come down here and fight me! If he kills me, then we will be your slaves. But if I kill him, you will be our slaves! I defy the armies of Israel today! Send me a man who will fight me!' When Saul and the Israelites heard this, they were terrified and deeply shaken." (NLT)

What circumstances in your life have made you shrink in fear like King Saul and his men?

Too often, instead of facing a fearful life situation with courage, we run from it. We cringe in fear over things we hear. A bad report. A dire diagnosis. A dreaded phone call. A rejected application. A starting spot, spurned. A client, lost. A promotion, denied. A spouse, departed.

When a giant speaks impossibility into our lives, and we are silent, we are weakened. We have no strength to stand.

In our biblical story, the armies of Israel stood paralyzed by a giant called fear for forty days. Forty wasted days. Forty lost opportunities. Afraid. Dressed for battle but mired in defeat. Fear is a potent killer. It parks you on a hill of passivity and is often fueled by those closest to you.

What if we were weren't afraid to face giants? What if we ran to the Goliaths in our industry? What if we refused to be intimidated by things bigger than us? Goliath was mightier in strength than David. He was an experienced warrior. David, although a warrior, was young and inexperienced. Yet against all odds, against all human wisdom, strength and credentials, God gave him a victory no one saw coming.

There will always be someone taller, prettier, more experienced, or educated than we are. But none of these qualities guarantee success, and the lack of them doesn't disqualify us. Yes, in life, there will always be a Goliath, but God is calling us to be giant killers. He's calling us to cut the head (authority) off every giant impeding us from living out our dreams.

The apostle Paul faced many giants during his ministry. Yet he was able to write: "And do not [for a moment] be frightened or intimidated in anything by your opponents and adversaries, for such [constancy and fearlessness] will be a clear sign (proof and seal) to them of [their impending] destruction, but [a sure token and evidence] of your deliverance and salvation, and that from God" (Philippians 1:28 AMP).

Paul wrote the book of Philippians while he was in prison, his giant at the time. But Paul used his imprisonment to make Christ known. He constructed a pulpit out of his problems and refused to let giants intimidate him (v. 20).

Likewise, every calling we have, every relationship we build, every job we take, every business we start, and every dream in our heart will face at least one giant—and maybe more.

Goliath taunted Israel's right to be in battle with him, shouting, "Give me a man," until a boy emerged. David was the unlikeliest of heroes. Unknown. Under six feet. Young and inexperienced. But small people can do big things for God. David was anointed to be king, so he ran to his Goliath. And the reward was this: Whatever happened in the life of the victor would happen to his people.

Hero stories, whether historical or fantasy, have always been rooted in this principle. As a huge Marvel and DC movie fan, I have seen it time after time:

- Whatever happened to the Guardians, happened to the Galaxy
- Whatever happened to Superman happened to Metropolis
- Whatever happened to Batman happened to Gotham
- Whatever happened to Spider-Man happened to New York and the world.

Likewise, whatever happened to Jesus happened to us. When He died on the cross, we died with Him. When He was buried, every trace of our tormenting past was buried with Him. When He was resurrected, we too were raised to new resurrection life. We are now seated with Him far above principalities, powers, thrones, and dominions.

The apostle Paul prayed for the church in Ephesus:

I pray that your hearts will be flooded with light so that you can understand the confident hope he has given to those he called—his holy people who are his rich and glorious inheritance. I also pray that you will understand the incredible greatness of God's power for us who believe him. This is the same mighty power that raised Christ from the dead and seated him in the place of honor at God's right hand in the heavenly realms. Now he is far above any ruler or authority or power or leader or anything else, not only in this world but also in the world to come. God has put all things under the authority of Christ and has made him head over all things for the benefit of the church. And the church is his body; it is made full and complete by Christ, who fills all things everywhere with himself. (Ephesians 1:18-23 NLT)

Jesus Is Our Giant Killer

Jesus didn't come to make a truce with the enemy. He came to defeat him and make us winners. Our lives don't have to resemble a tie or defeat. Despite the losing or winning percentage, past failures and losses, we are called to be champions in our generation, champions of something bigger than we are (*e.g.*, a champion of human rights, cancer, depression, anger, or mental health). Christ came to impart heroism to our life—to transform us from victim to victor. From coward to giant killer. We are greater than labels others put on us. Where giants have made us

23

feel small, God's love makes us great. He increases and enlarges us to do impossible things.

When you look at the biggest dream in your heart, the position you want, the stage you want to glorify God with, is it filled with people who are bigger, more powerful, with more endorsements, credentials, wins, and experience?

No problem.

Goliath was stronger than any Israelite soldier. The Israelites showed up in battle ranks for forty days, dressed for battle, but with no intent to fight or engage the enemy. They were imposters. Because what happened to Saul happened to them.

Repeatedly, Saul made decisions based on the fear of man. He thought sacrifice was better than obedience. In 1 Samuel 13:7-12, we read:

Meanwhile, Saul stayed at Gilgal, and his men were trembling with fear. Saul waited there seven days for Samuel, as Samuel had instructed him earlier, but Samuel still didn't come. Saul realized that his troops were rapidly slipping away. So he demanded, "Bring me the burnt offering and the peace offerings!" And Saul sacrificed the burnt offering himself. Just as Saul was finishing with the burnt offering, Samuel arrived. Saul went out to meet and welcome him, but Samuel said, "What is this you have done?" (NLT)

Saul's fear of man entered through the door of his troops' lives. Human fear, influence, and opinion cheated him out of his throne. What happened to Saul happened to his men in front of Goliath. Whatever happens to us affects those who look to us for influence—our children, our extended family, or those we lead in business, school, or ministry.

Fear Steals Destiny and Dreams

Fear is a thief. It steals hope. It robs us of our best years, our best dreams. It strips what is owed to our generation. But God's perfect love can drive it out. He is still big enough to accomplish the biggest dream in our heart. God took a boy anointed in private, not chosen in public, to slay a giant. He took David's private devotion—and anointing—to guide the stone that killed Goliath. There is no battle to win in public, until you win the war raging in private.

In the chapters that follow, we'll focus on seven giants or dream killers. Seven is God's number of perfection. God jumped over seven brothers to choose David—a man after His own heart—to defeat Goliath.

As thrilling as the victory was, we see David's incredible perspective in facing giants. He told King Saul: "The LORD who rescued me from the claws of the lion and the bear will *rescue* me from this Philistine!" (1 Samuel 17:37 NLT).

Likewise, the giant we face is God's opportunity to rescue us. To rescue failed or broken dreams that have died in the shadow of Goliath. That word *rescue* means, "To free or deliver from any confinement, violence, danger or evil; to liberate from actual restraint; to remove or withdraw from a state of exposure to evil" (*Dictionary.com*).

While imprisoned, the apostle Paul wrote to Timothy:

> Stir up (rekindle the embers of, fan the flame of, and keep burning) the [gracious] gift of God, [the inner fire] that is in you by means of the laying on of my hands [with those of the elders at your ordination]. For God did not give us a spirit of timidity (of cowardice, of craven and cringing and fawning fear), but [He has given us a spirit] of power and of love and of calm and well-balanced mind and discipline and self-control. (2 Timothy 1:6-7 AMP)

The Holy Spirit is a gift of God that is not shaken but stirred. Paraphrased, Paul told Timothy, "Don't live in the shadow of your mom's anointing. Stir up the fire—the dreams—the call of God that is in you. Awaken the giant killer within. God didn't give you the spirit of a coward. He gave you the spirit to win—to be a champion."

Nobody's Perfect

God wants to rescue us from our giants, to save us from the pressure of being perfect. David was not perfect. He committed adultery with Bathsheba. He impregnated her and killed her husband. Yet out of that flawed and failed lineage and transformation, Christ was birthed. You and I are not perfect, but because God's love for us is complete, He can make us something our parents were not. His love is powerful to change and transform any problem into a platform—to make us generational giant killers.

Despite David's sins with Bathsheba and all his imperfections and failures, God told his son, Solomon, "As for you, if you will follow me with integrity and godliness, as David your father did, obeying all my commands, decrees, and regulations, then I will establish the throne of your dynasty over Israel forever" (1 Kings 9:1-5 NLT).

Deeply flawed, David still had a legacy of influence with his son. Why? Because God sees us differently from what has been spoken by other people. People may remember how we failed in our past, but God watches how we walk with Him throughout our entire lifetime. His plan, purpose, and will for our lives prevails. He formed every bone and organ in our body. Shaped us from nothing into something. Understands our thoughts that are afar off.

Yet God is always thinking and speaking about the best He sees in you and me. He is crazy about us. Every single moment He thinks of you. His desires—His dreams for your life are more than the sand on the seashore.

He longs to give us hope that, in spite of who we were, we can still inspire the next generation with who we are now. God can add value to the wasted years of our lives. He is the great restorer.

It's incredible how, when valuable, people will come after us. But value must first be proved. When auto manufacturers make a new product, it goes to a testing or beta stage (for instance, crash-test dummies). After the car passes the test, the manufacturers then create mottos based on the success (*e.g.*, Ford – "Built Tough...#1 in Safety").

When we were born, we were untested in life. We had to go through some crash tests to prove the value we didn't know existed. Often, God will test us through dumb decisions we make before He allows us to affect real lives. He makes us something we currently are not. Gives beauty for ashes. Joy from defeat. Strength in pain when we least expect it.

Seasons of Testing

In 1996, I became a member of Melodyland Christian Center in Anaheim, California. I was introduced to Pastor Ralph Wilkerson by the late Reverend Jimmie McDonald. After spending my entire life serving in my mom's church, this change was initially hard. I had to start all over again in ministry, unlearning and relearning some things. When Pastor Ralph retired, he passed the leadership of the church to Pastors Neville and Wendy McDonald from South Africa. It had been my dream to be hired full-time on the pastoral staff, but this didn't happen. It seemed I was always the third-string quarterback—the last choice.

When we would lose youth pastors, I would fill in on an interim basis, only to see the church hire someone else for the position. From 1998, they hired four youth pastors over me. One of them, after leaving,—would mock me, stating, "Are you still working for free at the church?" I would often lament, "Why can't they see my value?" Then one day God spoke to my heart: "Son, show them how you are valuable." Then, my perspective changed. I realized promotion doesn't come from the east or west, but from God (Psalm 75:6).

During my time at the church, I led worship, pastored youth groups, acted in productions, counseled members, married and buried people, preached sermons, and eventually became an associate pastor and board member. They offered me a salary, which I turned down initially because the church could not afford it. God became my compensation. He was my hope and great reward. This season of testing taught me: "Man shall not live on bread alone, but on every word that comes from the mouth of God" (Matthew 4:4 NIV). In those years, I learned a valuable lesson: Sometimes we sow in one place but reap in another. Everything I poured into my church, God gave back to me somewhere else—in wisdom, faith, experience, favor, business clients, etc.

The apostle Paul wrote to the church in Rome: "Can anything ever separate us from Christ's love? Does it mean He no longer loves us if we have trouble or calamity, or are persecuted, or hungry, or destitute, or in danger, or threatened with death? No, despite all these things, overwhelming victory is ours through Christ, who loved us" (Romans 8:35, 37 NLT).

No giant Paul ever faced could defeat him. Paul knew he was more than a conqueror. He was a champion. Every one of us needs to know that truth and live in it.

Be Willing to March

Years ago, when I walked the Revlon Cancer Walk, I was amazed at seeing more than 40,000 people marching to fight something society says is incurable. The world's oldest documented case of cancer hails from ancient Egypt in 1500 B.C. Yet here, centuries later, every marcher was raising money to defeat it. Refusing to give up, they continued their fight in the memory of those who had succumbed to the disease. Inspired by lives close to them, they fought on.

Are you a fighter? Are you marching against things that people say are incurable in your life? Don't diminish your life's worth because of the past. Despite your history, you can still leave a legacy. Stop repeating the thought patterns of previous generations.

Today, Goliath is mocking your best life. Don't listen to him. Don't let him steal your dreams. Don't be afraid to:

- Silence the voice of your giant.
- Pursue your dream.
- Finish the book God has called you to write.
- Achieve the goals you have set.
- Start the business you've been procrastinating over.
- Restore your broken relationships.
- Recover from mistakes—don't carry them one more day.
- Love, forgive, or repair breaches in your life.

God put those dreams in your heart. He knows there is a giant killer inside of you. Now you must live it out, take God at His word, and run towards it.

For forty days, God was waiting for a generation to respond to Goliath.

That generation, my friend, is you.

CHAPTER 2

THE SEVEN GIANTS PRESENT

The Bible recounts another episode involving giants. In Deuteronomy 7:1-2, God told his children:

> When the LORD your God brings you into the land you are about to enter and occupy, he will clear away many nations ahead of you: the Hittites, Girgashites, Amorites, Canaanites, Perizzites, Hivites, and Jebusites. These seven nations are greater and more numerous than you. When the LORD your God hands these nations over to you and you conquer them, you must completely destroy them. Make no treaties with them and show them no mercy." (NLT)

The Israelites had to conquer seven nations to achieve their highest dream, the Promised Land. They couldn't hide from the giants. They couldn't pray them away. They couldn't wait for God to drown them. They had to drive them out of the place God had commanded them to occupy. No mercy. These seven nations were literal people in the past, but now represent seven giants, strongmen, or spirits we can harbor in our hearts today.

Defined, these seven nations were:

The Hittites: Sons of terror. Hidden torments. Phobias. Depression. Deceit.

The Girgashites: Clay dwellers. Focus on earthliness. Dissatisfaction. Unbelief in the unseen.

The Amorites: Mountain people. Renowned. Obsession with earthly fame, glory, and dictatorship.

The Canaanites: Lowlands people. Addictions. Perversions. A desire to please others with base values.

The Perizzites: Belonging to a village. Limited vision or dreams. Laziness. Low self-esteem.

The Hivites: Villagers. Vision is limited to enjoying an earthly inheritance—the pursuit of pleasure. Sensual self-indulgence.

The Jebusites: Threshers. Suppression of spiritual authority and potential in others. Legalism.

These are the seven giants you will face in life.

When the Israelites arrived at the doorstep of what God promised, the land of Canaan, and saw these giants, they wouldn't go in. In Numbers 13:18-20, Moses commanded twelve men of the tribes to scout the land to see what the giants' weaknesses and strengths were and to see if this was a good, fertile, and fat land. These men were to find out if these inhabitants lived in camps or strongholds. Were there resources, like timber, for building? Was the fruit of the land all God said it was? You'll find their scouting report to Moses in Numbers 13:27-33:

We entered the land you sent us to explore, and it is indeed a bountiful country—a land flowing with milk and honey. Here is the kind of fruit it produces. But the people living there are powerful, and their towns are large and fortified. We even saw giants there, the descendants of Anak! The Amalekites live in the Negev, and the Hittites, Jebusites, and Amorites live in the hill country. The Canaanites live along the coast of the Mediterranean Sea and along the Jordan Valley." But Caleb tried to quiet the people as they stood before Moses. "Let's go at once to take the land," he said. "We can certainly conquer it!" But the other men who had explored the land with him disagreed. "We can't go up against them! They are stronger than we are!" So they spread this bad report about the land among the Israelites: "The land we traveled through and explored will devour anyone who goes to live there. All the people we saw were huge. We even saw giants there, the descendants of Anak. Next to them we felt like grasshoppers, and that's what they thought, too! (NLT)

Think about it. Ten people with a bad report. Only ten spies, because of their fear of giants, resulted in more than two million people dying with dreams still in them. A twelve-man jury, sequestered for forty days, issued a verdict that would result in a false conviction shattering thousands of families.

The scouting data was never meant to intimidate or defeat them. It was to inspire strategy and battle plans. But the Israelites failed to execute a plan. Too often, we allow data or a bad report to drive us to defeat instead of a strategy. But no team, preparing for a game, scouts an opposing team to quit. They scout the opposition to gain a winning edge. To figure out the opponent's weaknesses. To improve the team's chances to win and game-plan their victory. Giants distracted God's people from seeing any of these. They allowed fear to keep them in a place of safety and of wandering forty years on the doorstep of their dreams.

Here, the giants in the land forced two distinct responses:

1. FEAR. Ten men came back with a false report: "We can't attack them. They are of great size. They are stronger than us. They are too powerful. We feel small and insignificant in their presence" (Numbers 13:27-33, author paraphrase).
2. DEFIANCE. Two men came back with a defiant perspective:

Joshua son of Nun and Caleb son of Jephunneh, who were among those who had explored the land, tore their clothes and said to the entire Israelite assembly, "The land we passed through and explored is exceedingly good. If the Lord is pleased with us, he will lead us into that land, a land flowing with milk and honey, and will give it to us. Only do not rebel against the Lord. And do not be afraid of the people of the land, because we will devour them. Their protection is gone, but the Lord is with us. Do not be afraid of them." (Numbers 14:6-9 NLT)

Sometimes God makes a promise to you that seems impossible. But on the other side of your greatest fear, your best life is waiting. These ten spies convinced millions of people to fear giants, not realizing the entire city of Jericho had been afraid of the Israelites for thirty-eight years:

Before the spies went to sleep that night, Rahab went up on the roof to talk with them. "I know the LORD has given you this land," she told them. "We are all afraid of you. Everyone in the land is living in terror. For we have heard how the LORD made a dry path for you through the Red Sea when you left Egypt. And we know what you did to Sihon and Og, the two Amorite kings east of the Jordan River, whose people you completely destroyed. No wonder our hearts have melted in fear! No one has the courage to fight after hearing such things. For the LORD your God is the supreme God of the heavens above and the earth below. (Joshua 2:8-11 NLT)

Thirty-eight years later, the giants in Jericho were still talking about the Red Sea drowning of Pharaoh and his army. They were still melting in fear because of the Israelites.

The Place of Our Greatest Unbelief

On November 18, 1978, my family's life was drastically turned upside down, as one man, cult leader Jim Jones, ordered the assassination of Congressmen Leo Ryan and the deaths of more than 900 people, including more than 300 children. Before the mass murders in Jonestown, active shooters showed up at the Port Kaituma airstrip and killed Congressman Ryan, three members of his news crew, and one defector from the People's Temple Commune. The shooting triggered the mass murder-suicide of more than 900 people shortly thereafter. The sting of their senseless deaths, and what they could have become, still haunts many today. Before the terrorist attacks of September 11, 2001, the tragedy at Jonestown marked the most significant loss of U.S. civilian life in a non-natural disaster. The terrorists on 9/11 used planes to kill more than 3,000 people. Jim Jones used false dreams and fear to kill his members. Although not members, my mother and I lost twenty-seven relatives (including my grandmother) that day. I would have been one of them, but my mom hid me when I was six years old because she began to have prophetic dreams that Jim Jones was going to kidnap children and kill our family in a jungle. Her obedience to this vision saved me from a kidnapping plot that claimed several of my close cousins.

I vividly remember the night before my grandma fled to Jonestown. Her departure came on the heels of a bad argument with my late aunt. My grandmother had given candy to my cousin, which caused him to get sick. A thrown milk carton exploded against the wall. Harsh words ensued. It became physical—one of those altercations you wished had not happened. Afterward, my grandma walked painfully to her room. I followed close behind and found her weeping. I grabbed her around her waist as she pulled a suitcase out and packed it to leave to a place, she thought was better than America.

I never saw her again.

What Makes Us Run?

What is it in life that makes us run from our purpose, problems, people, and even our destiny? We run because we are afraid. We fear life remaining the same or changing. We fear the past repeating itself. We fear people hurting us again. We fear what is unknown. We fear trusting people. We fear disappointing them and not having the ability to get the job done. Not being good enough. Pretty enough. Accepted. Adequate. Understood. We fear all kinds of things: success, failure, small places, heights, public speaking, dentists, sickness, death, and so on. Our sources of fear are endless.

We're brimming with talent, purpose, and potential, but we lack the fearlessness and faith to release it. Sight has failed us. But God told Joshua: "If you dare walk on what you are afraid of and come out of the shadows of your biggest giants and critics, there won't be a wall big enough to contain the blessing and increase in your life. I'll give you the territory you are afraid of" (Joshua 1:1-9, author's paraphrase).

Joshua and Caleb had God-ordained faith for a God-ordained moment, yet were deprived of their destiny for forty years because ten people feared giants.

What are you afraid of in life?

More than 900 people died in Jonestown because they feared one man.

What happened to my family in 1978 happens to the best of us today. We run from problems. We fail. We make mistakes. We stay in comfort zones. We ignore red flags. We cower in shame and guilt. We fear change. We get misunderstood. We fight bouts of depression. We ignore symptoms. We stay in unhealthy, abusive, familiar, and yet sometimes destructive relationships out of fear. We die prematurely taking our dreams to the grave. We refuse to face and defeat our giants.

The late Myles Munroe once said, "The poorest man in the world is the man without a dream. The most frustrated man in the world is the man with a dream that never becomes a reality." In Oakland, California, at The

Evergreen Cemetery, there is a mass grave of 412 uniden-
tified bodies—412 dreams that died in Jonestown.

One of the greatest myths is that Jonestown was a
mass suicide. It was not. It was mass murder. Stanley
Clayton, a cult survivor, told the *Chicago Tribune* that cult
members were surrounded by armed guards and forced to
take poison. Jim Jones was a diabolical giant. But there
were undoubtedly some lost souls who took their lives for
the "cause."

What was the deplorable condition in Jonestown that
led *some* to the grim decision to end it all? Some of the
survivors reported upon return to America that things
were so bad that my grandma, who fled there, tried to kill
Jim Jones with a machete. Why do people take their own
lives? What makes us treat suicide differently based on
who the victim was? For example, why was the public
response so different to the losses of Robin Williams, Kate
Spade, and Anthony Bourdain to that of Aaron Hernandez,
former tight end for the New England Patriots? Because
people remember how we lived, regardless of how we die.

Family Life Today recently interviewed Albert Hsu,
the author of *Grieving a Suicide,* who has lost his own
father to suicide. Hsu shared that one therapist reported
how families of these victims are often found in graveyards
screaming at tombstones of their dead loved ones because
suicide heightens the grief over a loved one's death. They
are angry. They are hurt. They can't blame a drunk driver.
They can't blame a natural disaster. They can't blame a

disease. They have to look to questions like "What could I have done differently?" or "Could I have done more?"

Don't get to the end of your life asking these questions. Don't take your dreams and potential to the grave. Jesus gave up His life, to raise yours. He stripped Himself of all privileges and rights, so nothing would have the power to take yours. In John 10:10, He said: "The thief comes only in order to steal and kill and destroy. I came that they may have and enjoy life, and have it in abundance (to the full, till it [a]overflows). (AMP). Jesus died to make life worth living.

When God gave us Jesus, He was the stone to the head of every Goliath we would face. He came to fulfill what the law or men could not do. He fulfills the failed acquisition of past promises in our present lives. He is the perfect image of the courage the ten spies lacked to face giants. The perfect image of a giant killer. A King. A Father of faith. A vow keeper. A deliverer. An ark builder. An Isaac to be sacrificed. A second Adam.

When we let Him live in us, no matter what our old or first life looks like, He can make all things new. He can help us conquer our giants—the obstacles in life that are massive in proportion to us. Every promise broken by men can be restored by Jesus. No unmet need will prevail against us. No giant will lie and convince us to die prematurely. Our dreams will live. We will declare the works of God to predict our outcome because we have been given the greatest treasure, Jesus—our giant killer, dwelling in us.

Kill your Goliath.

CHAPTER 3

THE GIANT OF FEAR

Hittites*: Sons of terror. Hidden torments. Phobias. Depression. Deceit.*

Have you ever been terrorized at the thought of being attacked while walking home at night? Fearful that your children will go down the wrong path? That you will die of a terminal disease? Lose your job and face unemployment? That your spouse will leave you?

The first enemy God commanded the Israelites to confront was fear, which is represented in Scripture by the Hittites. God told His children:

> Perhaps you will think to yourselves, "How can we ever conquer these nations that are so much more powerful than we are?" But don't be afraid of them! Just remember what the LORD your God did to Pharaoh and to all the land of Egypt. Remember the great terrors the LORD your God sent against them. You saw it all with your own eyes! And remember the miraculous signs and wonders, and

the strong hand and powerful arm with which he brought you out of Egypt. The LORD your God will use this same power against all the people you fear." (Deuteronomy 7:17-19 NLT)

Terror is the extreme manifestation of fear.

The Hittites were the warlike element of this confederation of seven tribes. They were a Hamitic race and called "the sons of Heth," whose name means "terror." A Hittite is one who keeps you from stepping out into an unknown place. A Hittite represents hidden torments you don't want people to know exist in your life. It's a giant that terrorizes you through fear. It is something your emotions feed on to bring you down. It will keep you out of the place God has called you to possess. It will discredit your identity in Christ and twist itself in whatever way necessary to consume your thoughts.

I was first exposed to the People's Temple cult as a child by my grandmother, who kept me while my mom, Dr. Jynona Norwood, traveled for ministry. When visiting the Temple, it was easy to see why so many followed Jim Jones. I can't remember a time where there were not free toys and food available. Jones filled unmet needs, coming into the African American community strategically during a time of poverty and racial inequality. My mother vehemently fought Jim Jones and asked her mother and grandmother not to take me to the Temple, but they didn't listen.

One day, upon my mother's return from a trip, I remember her coming and pulling me out of the Temple while Jim Jones's leaders held onto my other arm in a human tug-a-war. My mom eventually hid me in Daly City, California, as a strong response to her fears and the prophetic dreams God showed her. She took steps to make sure I was safe. She saw Jim Jones for who he was—a divisive tyrant creating isolation and a fear of punishment among his followers.

Jones would subject his members to physical beatings and public humiliation to cultivate this atmosphere of fear. I remember visiting the Temple when I was around six or seven. It was a morning service, and you could sense something wrong as there was an eerie, chilling feeling in the air. Later, Jones would have his followers create a boxing ring out of the stage to reprimand a five-year-old boy who had accidentally broken a little girl's leg while playing. The punishment: three rounds in the ring with an eight-year-old boy who pounded him into unconsciousness while some members cheered, but others watched in horror.

In the article "Inside People's Temple," Marshall Kilduff and Phil Tracy write:

According to Elmer and Deanna Mertles (formerly Al and Jeanne Mills), who left the Temple and exposed Jim Jones, one night their daughter Linda was called up for discipline because she had hugged and kissed a woman friend she hadn't seen in a long time. The woman was reputed to be a lesbian. The Mertles stood among the congregation of 600 or 700 while their daughter, who was then sixteen, was hit on her buttocks 75 times. "She was beaten so severely," said Elmer, "that the kids said her butt looked like a hamburger." Linda later testified of the beating, "I couldn't sit down for at least a week and a half."

Jones was a false prophet and manipulator who preyed on underserved people with dreams—the abandoned, the fatherless, the hopeless, even the hopeful. He preached sermons that echoed Dr. Martin Luther King. He appeared with mayors, governors, and presidents. He deceived everybody. In 1976, Mayor George Moscone appointed Jones to the San Francisco Housing Authority, where he eventually became the chair. Many considered him a saint, but he was the spirit of the anti-Christ. He was the epitome of the false prophets described in 2 Peter 2, which come to secretly infiltrate the church in the last days.

In his message, "Let the Night Roar," Jones spewed a profanity-laden message that love is not the only weapon. He incited members to use whatever weapon they could to kill those who would oppose "the cause." He weaponized destructive ways of thinking—outrageous behavior, greed, division of families, cunning arguments, slandered truth, false freedom—to bait his members into a life against God.

Jones threw the Bible down. Stomped on it. Created an atmosphere of terror and intimidation in the hearts of his people. In short, he represented a Hittite giant. When a Hittite is present, a sense of chaos, purposelessness, and emptiness will invade your life. It will try to bring intense distress to you. A Hittite is a demon of extreme fear. It seeks to undermine or make you second-guess your dream. It relentlessly seeks the death of what is inside of you.

Here are a few people in Scripture who battled the Hittite or giant of fear:

- Elijah, the prophet, sat under a juniper tree and wanted to die (1 Kings 18-19 NLT).
- Jeremiah, the prophet, sat on a hill, depressed and weeping over the devastation of his beloved city (Lam 3:14-20 NLT).
- Rebekah, Jacob's mother, lamented, "If Jacob marries a daughter of Heth, what good will my life be to me?" (Gen. 26:34, 27:46 NLT).

The Fear of Man Destroys Dreams

In Genesis 25, Rebekah receives a prophetic word from God, but immediately in the next chapter, she declares she wants to die. The Hittite giant preys on the vulnerability of emotions and whispers speculation into your heart: What if you don't make it? What if you fail? What if you never get married? What if your idea never works? What if there is a complication? What if the cancer spreads? What if you die? What if this is the farthest you can go?

Sometimes as parents, we sacrifice and mortgage ourselves to make our children's dreams come to pass while failing to leave a legacy of what it looks like to conquer Jericho. For years, I achieved some goals, defeated some giants, but not all of them. I was doing good, but not great. The fact that you are reading this book is evidence that one of my giants, procrastination, has fallen. While praying for a book deal and traveling to speaking engagements, I would pass airport bookstands and envision *Be a Giant Killer* displayed on the stands. But I did not want to write it just for the sake of writing a book. I wanted to tell my story. I wanted to write something to inspire heart change that would not merely have an impact on readers, but on dreams and future generations.

I finally completed this book after realizing my giant of procrastination could grow into the next generation. If my sons or daughter didn't see me pursue all of my dreams while at home, I would deprive them of the blueprint for accomplishing theirs. I would be like Moses, who led them to the doorstep, but could not take them in.

Fatal Attraction

Michael Prokes, a 31-year-old main spokesperson and press contact for the Temple, killed himself four months after escaping Jonestown with a large suitcase of money. In the days before his suicide, Prokes composed a thirty-page statement about the People's Temple, writing:

> The 'total dedication' you once observed of me was not to Jim Jones, it was to an organization of people who had nothing left to lose. No matter what view

one takes of the Temple, perhaps the most rele-
vant truth is that it was filled with outcasts and
the poor who were looking for something they
could not find in our society. ... And sadly enough,
there are millions more out there with all kinds
of different, but desperate needs whose lives will
end tragically, as happens every day. No matter
how you cut it, you just can't separate Jonestown
from America, because the People's Temple was
not born in a vacuum, and despite the attempt to
isolate it, neither did it end in one.

Michael Prokes died because of a fatal attraction. Jim
Jones deceived these kinds of dreamers and even made
some of them sick murderers. He took advantage of the
hurting, oppressed, sick, hopeless, abused, vibrant, intel-
ligent, poor, and even wealthy, who were filled with potential. He rehabilitated addicts. He fought for equality and
social justice for those discriminated against. He took
fatherless children into his arms. He tricked more than
900 people into running away from their problems, from
the people who did not understand them or believe what
they believed. They ran until they arrived at a place of
no return. Then in 1978, he killed them. He assassinated
Congressman Leo Ryan, who came to investigate human
rights violations, then ordered the deaths of those in the
commune called Jonestown.

The No Timid Zone

We need boldness to face giants or circumstances bigger than we are. The Christian life is a life of courage: a life of growth that involves conviction, follow through (even at great cost), and ruthless honesty in the presence of God, so that we are constantly transformed and unrecognizable to people who knew us as we used to be.

The people of Jonestown wanted a quick fix.

Sometimes in this drive-through society, we want immediate deliverance but not the process of becoming a great nation. A great husband. Wife. Mother. Father. A successful entrepreneur. A healed man or woman of faith. A giant killer. But everything the Israelites went through in Egypt was to move them from a favored position, to a hated one, then to the promise. After Moses died, God told Joshua:

No one will be able to stand against you as long as you live. For I will be with you as I was with Moses. I will not fail you or abandon you. "Be strong and courageous, for you are the one who will lead these people to possess all the land I swore to their ancestors I would give them. Be strong and very courageous. Be careful to obey all the instructions Moses gave you. Do not deviate from them, turning either to the right or to the left. Then you will be successful in everything you do. Study this Book of Instruction continually. Meditate on it day and night so you will be sure to obey everything written in it. Only then will you prosper and succeed in all you do. This is my command—be strong and courageous! Do not be afraid or discouraged. For the LORD your God is with you wherever you go. (Joshua 1:5-9 NLT)

Rephrased, God said, "Do not be timid in what I have called you to be. Do not be timid in walking where I have put you. Act like you belong as the new leader. Don't lead or live in the grief of what has died in your life. Live. Walk on your promise. Knock down walls. Conquer your fears, and you will fulfill your destiny!"

In the Bible, no one who was timid ever possessed anything. The apostle Paul wrote to Timothy concerning his calling and said, "For the Spirit God gave us does not make us timid, but gives us power, love and self-discipline. So do not be ashamed of the testimony about our Lord or of me his prisoner. Rather, join with me in suffering for the gospel, by the power of God" (2 Timothy 1:7-8 NIV).

Paul also wrote, "Whatever you are called to do, do it in the power of God"—not in the power of human strength. Paul inspired the church by planting churches and writing 80% of the New Testament, yet he made statements like: "I am the least of all the saints" (Ephesians 3:8-9) and "I am the least of the apostles" (1 Corinthians 15:9-11). Paul did not separate his business from ministry. He recognized he was what he was because of the grace of God. He wanted to make sure this grace was not in vain. He labored by the grace of God to make sure that his life's work (*e.g.*, church planting and building, preaching, making tents) brought men into a saving knowledge of who Christ was.

A few years ago, I spoke at a healthcare conference, and afterward one of the attendees said they felt a "wonderful presence" and that "the only thing missing was an altar call." Why? Because every time people come to hear me speak, I want them to feel the love of Jesus, no matter what I am talking about.

My companies were founded on Romans 15:21 (AMP), where the apostle Paul said, "But [instead I would act on the principle] as it is written, 'They shall see who have never been told of Him, and they shall understand who have never heard [of Him].'" For twenty years, I have asked God to show me how to use kingdom principles to reach not only church congregations but also general audiences because I genuinely believe our greatest place of influence is our ministry.

Does your humility, your best work, show Jesus to men and women in your circle of influence? To be great in anything, you have to reckon yourself the least of all. Undeserving. Unworthy. Then you won't get full of yourself or puffed up. We are called to rely totally on God to be effective and see our dreams come to pass. It doesn't matter if you blow an opportunity along the way. We all do that. Just remember, God set a precedent to a thousand generations. Even if you blow it and wander thirty-eight years in a wilderness of bad decisions, He can still do what He promised (See Psalm 89:30-34). In Genesis 8:18,

Noah built an altar on the gravesite of his giants. He made redemptive decisions in the place of bad ones.

In life, we can't escape problems (or Hittites) by running from them. But we can be problem solvers. Hope bringers. We can slay the Hittite. We can be something the enemy never intended us to be.

So What Shall We Be?

The apostle John wrote, "Dear friends, now we are children of God, and *what we will be* has not yet been made known. But we know that when Christ appears, we shall be like him, for we shall see him as he is" (1 John 3:2 NIV, emphasis added).

We don't always understand how present circumstances relate to what we shall be. We don't always comprehend the gravity of the moment or season we're in, or how what we're going through will produce something exceptional. So, we run. We run away from God to isolation. Fear. Passivity. Addiction. Depression.

The apostle Paul, who was falsely imprisoned, stoned, shipwrecked, bitten by a viper, and beaten thirty-nine times, wrote: "For our present troubles are small and won't last very long. Yet they produce for us a glory that vastly outweighs them and will last forever! So we don't look at the troubles we can see now; rather, we fix our gaze on things that cannot be seen. For the things we see now will soon be gone, but the things we cannot see will last forever" (2 Corinthians 4:17-18 NLT).

This giant moment is producing something in you, greater than anything you can imagine, dream, hope, or pray for.

You can defeat giants. You can be something your lineage has never seen before. You can be a thousand times more than what you currently are. You can defy your greatest fears. You can beat sickness, financial reverses, relationship breakups, unfair criticism, or anything else the enemy throws at you. The blood of Jesus is stronger than your history.

Whatever is lacking in our lives, God, by his Spirit, will strengthen, complete, and perfect us to make us what we ought to be. He makes us whole. He makes us righteous and new. He makes us fearless giant killers. Romans 8:19 says, "For all creation is waiting eagerly for that future day when God will reveal who his children really are" (NLT).

All of creation stands on tiptoes to see what you and I will do next.

Many people left to go Jonestown for reasons like my family did. They ran. When I think of the relatives I lost that day, including seven close cousins (one was only three months old), I shudder to think of all they missed. Spiritually, they missed out on fulfilling God's dreams for them. But they also missed out on things like:

- Video games
- Sony Walkmans
- Cellular phones
- Microsoft Windows

- The internet
- Superstars such as Michael Jordan, Whitney Houston, Lebron James, and Kobe Bryant.
- Dynasties such as their hometown San Francisco 49ers winning five Super Bowls, the NBA Championship Warriors who have won three championships, and Chicago Bulls winning six NBA Championships.
- Leather bomber jackets
- The iPod, Facebook, YouTube, and Twitter

And for the first time, an African American was sworn in as the president of the United States. That's what the 305 children of Jonestown could have experienced.

The Generational Gap

One-third of the victims in Jonestown were children.

Throughout Bible history, whenever Satan wanted to kill future generations, he tried to destroy the seed or children. King David wrote: "Through the praise of children and infants you have established a stronghold against your enemies, to silence the foe and the avenger" (Psalm 8:2 NIV).

Jim Jones lured people by what he provided for their children. Their parents were willing to walk in a jungle—a wilderness to give their children a promised utopia. A land of no hate, no racial profiling, no prejudice, no poverty. But the truth realized too late was that Jonestown was actually a living hell.

God still spares righteousness in a depraved world. Right decisions amid wrong ones. Sometimes God will reduce everything around you to ashes to save your life. In that jungle, died future inventors, professionals, moms and dads, future dreamers, and giant killers, so that we could learn from their losses.

What will you do with the next ten years of your life? What will you do with the dreams in your heart? We represent the living, breathing legacy of our generation. Many of us might have dreamed of being authors, artists, animators, professional athletes, entertainers, singers, heart surgeons, or president of the United States, but have failed to achieve it.

What will people see painted on the canvas of our lives?

In our constant search for identity or God's will for our life, we find comfort in knowing His ultimate plan is that we resemble Him. Above all else. Above all power. All fame. All careers. All aspirations. All NFL, NBA, and MLB dreams. All cures discovered. All art created. All music scored. All sermons preached. We are created for His glory.

Use Your Platform

In Luke 5, Jesus finds Peter after a career failure. Peter has spent the entire night fishing with no results, and Jesus arrives on the shore to ask, "Can I use what has failed in your life as a platform to glorify me? Can I use your failed efforts as a pulpit to speak into human lives?"

Afterwards, Jesus says:

"Now go out where it is deeper, and let down your
nets to catch some fish." "Master," Simon replied,
"we worked hard all last night and didn't catch
a thing. But if you say so, I'll let the nets down
again." And this time their nets were so full of fish
they began to tear! A shout for help brought their
partners in the other boat, and soon both boats
were filled with fish and on the verge of sinking.
When Simon Peter realized what had happened,
he fell to his knees before Jesus and said, "Oh,
Lord, please leave me—I'm such a sinful man."
For he was awestruck by the number of fish they
had caught, as were the others with him. His partners, James and John, the sons of Zebedee, were
also amazed. Jesus replied to Simon, "Don't be
afraid! From now on you'll be fishing for people!"
And as soon as they landed, they left everything
and followed Jesus. (vv.4-11 NLT)

God uses failure to redeem us powerfully.

Peter and his friends pulled their boats on the shore,
left everything, and followed Jesus. They left the wins
behind to pursue Him, to demonstrate that Jesus was more
important than accomplishments. Up to this point, Peter
has been using his boat to fish for money. But God wanted
him fishing for men.

Jesus illustrated to Peter that despite not seeing anything left—worth fishing for—there are plenty of fish in the sea. Peter had caught nothing all night, but Jesus knew there were plenty to catch.

Likewise, just because you haven't caught an opportunity or no one has come to Christ lately on your job or in your neighborhood or in your city, that doesn't mean you should abandon your dream (or sphere of influence). There are plenty of souls. Plenty of jobs. Plenty of fish in the sea.

Courage is putting down your nets, *at His word,* in a seemingly impossible place when everything screams, "leave!" or "move to another place."

I once told my son's football team during a devotional, "No matter if you are on scout team or first team, you must be tenacious. Tenacity will serve you in your lifetime. Players that endure and persevere will find a way to be successful no matter where they are or what they are doing. Don't quit!"

Tim Tebow, former Heisman Trophy winner and NFL player, hadn't played a snap in the league in years but was determined to use his fame for the glory of God. Years later, he had a baseball workout and the New York Mets signed him. Once he was at a minor league baseball game, a fan had a seizure and stopped breathing. Tim refused to leave. He was there for a reason. He laid his hands on the fan, who started breathing again.

What if he had not been there?

God knows exactly where we are. He created us for His glory not ours. But don't think He will expect anything less from us than He has from previous generations. We will confront the same giants the Israelites had to face. Giants that seek to crush our plans, hopes, and dreams, keeping us on the outer wall of what God promised. For thirty-eight years, the Israelites were afraid of what was on the other side of Jericho, not realizing the entire city was shut up or afraid because of them.

Now the gates of Jericho were tightly shut because the people were afraid of the Israelites. No one was allowed to go out or in. But the LORD said to Joshua, "I have given you Jericho, its king, and all its strong warriors. You and your fighting men should march around the town once a day for six days. Seven priests will walk ahead of the Ark, each carrying a ram's horn. On the seventh day you are to march around the town seven times, with the priests blowing the horns. When you hear the priests give one long blast on the rams' horns, have all the people shout as loud as they can. *Then the walls of the town will collapse*, and the people can charge straight into the town. (Joshua 6:1-5 NLT)

God had given the Israelites the keys to the city, but walls and giants kept them under a delusion the city wasn't theirs. Can you imagine the pessimistic chatter from the people in the camp? "Why would God give us a city with collapsed walls? Why would He give us land without protection? We should have just stayed in Egypt."

But the blessing and increase God intends for our lives (*e.g.*, career, business, ministry) is not designed to be contained by the walls men build around us. God wants to increase us so much that human walls won't be big enough to contain what He promised and giants won't keep us wandering in a desert.

What fear, terror, phobia, or depression stands between you and your dream? How many Hittites or extreme fears affect the way you work, take risks, trust teams, build vision, serve, and love people?

Declare today:

- This place is too small for me.
- I will dream.
- I will do the impossible.
- I will not remain stagnant for the rest of my life.
- My dream will humiliate the devil.

On the other side of your biggest fear, your best life is waiting.

Let's go inside.

CHAPTER 4

THE GIANT OF DISSATISFACTION

Girgashites: Clay dwellers. Focus on earthliness.
Dissatisfaction. Unbelief in what cannot be seen.

Have you ever had a perfect life suddenly collapse
around you?

I was married on May 3, 1997, at the extravagant
Crystal Cathedral in Garden Grove, California. It was
one of the greatest days of my life. The next day, my wife
and I flew off to Italy for a ten-day honeymoon and for
much-needed romance and relaxation. Two weeks after
returning my great-grandmother and father-in-law died
seven days apart.

I felt cursed.

I asked God "Why?" repeatedly but received no
answer. Soon after their deaths, I suffered a subsequent
loss of my business due to financial mistakes. Amid my
confusion, pain, and tears, I realized a great transforming
work taking place in my life and discovered where I was
living: the wilderness.

The wilderness represents a time of temporary confusion. It is a season of shaking. A place where you have no idea how you got there. Where you question God. Where all efforts, all ideas, all assumptions, plans, and connections fail. Alcohol can't lessen the pain. Reputation can't open doors. No one seems to care, and nothing works. When Moses led the children of Israel out of Egypt, God led them through the wilderness to humble and test them—to see if He could trust them with what He promised.

The wilderness was a place where they could neither sow nor reap. It was dry, unfamiliar, hot, and uncomfortable. A place where they had no other choice but to trust God. We find a story of their dissatisfaction with the provision of God in Exodus 16:15: "The Israelites were puzzled when they saw it. 'What is it?' they asked each other. They had no idea what it was.

And Moses told them, 'It is the food the Lord has given you to eat'" (NLT). Moses further explained in Deuteronomy 8:16, "He fed you with manna in the wilderness, a food unknown to your ancestors. He did this to humble you and test you for your own good" (NLT).

But the Israelites lived with a critical "What is this?" attitude when God gave them manna from heaven. The giant of dissatisfaction cost them their dreams. They hated the wilderness. They didn't want to be there. They felt the desert was a place of defeat. But it was a moment of destiny. It was the only place God had their full and undivided attention. It was a place where their will aligned to His and where they learned they had need of Him on another level.

- For Jonah, the fish that swallowed him during his rebellion represented the wilderness.
- For Joseph, the jail cell, where he served time as a falsely accused convict, forgotten by family and friends, represented the wilderness.
- For me, suffering the loss of my grandma, father-in-law, business, and material things was the wilderness.

God allowed everything to be taken away that occupied His place in my life. He kept blowing the wind of the wilderness until I was so broken there was nothing left to take. Until I was willing to offer it all to Him.

Fall in Love with the Process

Often, we want the promise but not the process. We complain about the manna and crave the things we left behind. We grieve what is lost instead of celebrating what is left. A key reason people went to Jonestown was Jones's promise to build a utopia on earth. But Jonestown was a graveyard of broken dreams. A nightmare Jim Jones tried to camouflage as paradise. It was as much a paradise as the mass gravesite they are buried in today.

Instead of forty years in the wilderness, the people of Jonestown followed Jim Jones to a modern-day wilderness in the jungles of South America, where they eventually died. They struggled with the Girgashite. This giant draws our attention only to things that are visible and temporary. The Girgashite giant influences analytical people to base their life's decisions solely on what they see. When they decide between job opportunities, they only consider how much more money they will make. Rarely do they consider if there is a sound church in the area to keep them and their family spiritually fed or if the enemy is trying to consume their service to family and God with work.

Jim Jones made the people of Jonestown fear staying in America. He ordered the liquidation of their assets to build a false dream on earth. In one sermon, he told his followers: "What you need to believe in is what you can see ... If you see me as your friend, I'll be your friend. If you see me as your father, I'll be your father, for those of you that don't have a father ... If you see me as your savior, I'll be your savior. If you see me as your God, I'll be your God....You're gonna help yourself, or you'll get no help! There's only one hope of glory; that's within you! Nobody's gonna come out of the sky! There's no heaven up there! We'll have to make heaven down here!"

In the hearts of his followers, there was a fear of uncertainty for the future, so Jones demanded the people of Jonestown build something that would rival heaven. The Girgashite giant makes us very literal, saying things like: "Whatever happens is just how it's supposed to be." "Whatever the diagnosis, that's what I have." "It is what it is."

The Girgashite giant makes us easily shaken by what we see or by the unknown. When the diagnosis is terminal. When a career or business is ending. When the marriage looks like it's headed for divorce. When it seems like you'll never get married. Never get healed. Never recover. Never pass the exam. Never make the team. Never be good enough. Never get the job or promotion. Never get the school loan. Then here comes the Girgashite giant, screaming and shouting things like: "You will never make it." "You'll die like this." "You're too small." "You're not pretty enough." "You are too inexperienced and unqualified." The Girgashite defies our every move, every single day. He intimidates us into thinking there is nothing we can do about our giant.

What made David different from Saul and his army when facing Goliath? All were believers. Warriors. Dressed and armed for battle. But David smelled like sheep. He was bold and unconventional. He used his weapons. Do you? In that dream, are you using Goliath as an opportunity to increase your vision and war strategy? When facing a giant, we must fight differently. We must fight like we have never fought before.

Be Unconventional

The Word of God arms us with unconventional weapons to fight giants. It raises our winning percentage against the enemy. Sometimes we feel like grasshoppers in the sight of giants. We are like David's brothers. Dressed for battle but doing nothing. Passive. Entitled. Shaken with fear. But David was different. He was confident in God. He didn't struggle with insecurities of being picked last by his earthly father. It didn't matter that his earthly father wasn't a king; his Heavenly Father was.

My father was never around when I grew up. He had several other children—one whom he named the identical birth name given to me. As a result, I never felt wanted by him. When I fathered children of my own, I sought to provide them with everything my father failed to give me. In August of 2000, as I launched my second business, people said, "If the business doesn't succeed in six months, shut it down, and get a full-time job." I could have used a father's voice and guidance at this time. But I told them, "Thank you for your love and concern, but we're not in this to fail (WNITTF). And I coined this acronym and applied it to many areas of my life. I branded it on company promotional gifts. When my marriage was struggling, my wife and I would tell each other "WNITTF." Come hell or high water, we will make it. (Jokingly, our pastor used to say, "Murder maybe, but divorce never.") When our business struggled, when banks said no, when health plans denied our provider member claims improperly, when doubt crept into our thoughts, we reminded ourselves, "WNITTF—We're Not in This to Fail!"

I am so glad my wife stuck with me during tough times. I was very independent and guarded when we were married. When everything around her screamed to leave, she stayed. She forgave. She built her home with wisdom. She helped build the man I am today. King Lemuel once wrote, "Who can find a virtuous and capable wife?" (Proverbs 31:10 NLT). I did in mine, Anu Norwood. She sees things I don't always see. She makes me a better husband, father, boss, man, and giant killer. Her love is the greatest gift God has given me and she is far more precious than anything I own.

Seeing Beyond Our Five Senses

People with a Girgashite in their lives can't see beyond their five senses. Dissatisfied with the hand of cards they've been dealt, they hate what they have been given in life. They despise the manna and refuse to learn how to trust God in difficult seasons. Struggling to get past injustices done to them in the past, they remain bound. Tormented. Territorial. Unwilling to let anyone near them to heal or alter their perception or point of reference.

In Matthew 8:28 we read, "When Jesus arrived on the other side of the lake, in the region of the Gadarenes, two men who were possessed by demons met him. They came out of the tombs and were so violent that no one could go through that area" (NLT). Girgashite giants dominated the territory so that no one was able to pass by. (See Deuteronomy 7:1).

The Girgashite giant is a place in our lives where we can't get past the injustice of what someone did or didn't do for us.

King David's son Absalom was infuriated at his half-brother Amnon for raping his sister Tamar. Yet he never said anything to Amnon. "And though Absalom never spoke to Amnon about this, he hated Amnon deeply because of what he had done to his sister." (2 Samuel 13:22 NLT). Absalom did not speak to his brother for two years. Then, in a fit of harbored rage, Absalom killed Amnon (verse 28). Absalom's anger turned to bitter, hostile, then deadly resentment.

Silent wars kill. Living estranged from those who hurt us does not relieve unresolved pain. It does not stop triggers—the reminders of what they did—from occurring in our heart. The triggers may decrease, but they can still be present when a person steps into our presence. Time did not heal my estrangement from my father. The truth is there are still some things I need to hear from him.

Time does not heal.

Jesus heals—through powerful transformation, repentance, and change.

Absalom was never the same after his sister Tamer was humiliated. After killing his half-brother Amnon, Absalom fled his father's presence for three years. But in 2 Samuel 14, David's heart still longed for his estranged son. Therefore, Joab sent a wise woman to pretend she was mourning a son who killed his brother and claiming family members wanted the son dead. But David showed mercy. "As surely as the Lord lives," he replied, "not a hair on your son's head will be disturbed" (v. 11 NLT).

She responded,

Why don't you do as much for the people of God as you have promised to do for me? You have convicted yourself in making this decision because you have refused to bring home your own banished son. All of us must die eventually. Our lives are like water spilled out on the ground, which cannot be gathered up again. But God does not just sweep life away; instead, he devises ways to bring us back when we have been separated from him." (2 Samuel 14:13-14 NLT)

Don't allow resentment and disappointment to keep you from devising ways to reconcile with those you love. Don't sweep relationships away. Yes, create emotional and professional boundaries that preserve "the best you" and protect your heart from reinjury. But don't banish people from your life. Don't take resentment to the grave. Don't be bitter. Don't drink poison from the cup people give you. We all must die. We are like water spilled on the ground. Be beautiful. Be a sweet, refreshing, and clear stream of water in the lives of people.

Under the Fair Credit Reporting Act (FCRA), most negative items must be removed from your credit report seven years from the first date of delinquency (see Deuteronomy 15:1). Every seven years, debts are erased. Likewise, we must release people from the debts they owe us. Release your mom and dad. Release your estranged spouse. Release that sibling. Ask God to heal the memory of what they did. For the sake of our kids, the next generation, we must do this. Remove the lifetime ban you have against people. Don't let the giant of resentment live. Choose to live free. Free from the pain of their thoughtlessness. Free from the pain of their sin. Free from the pain of their unapologetic response. Free from the triggers, thought patterns, and rituals that make us "act in."

Acting In

Acting "in," always results in acting "out." It has fatal consequences to the dreams in our heart.

Job 5:2 says, "Resentment kills a fool, and envy slays the simple" (NIV). King Solomon added, "Better is the end of a thing than the beginning of it, and the patient in spirit is better than the proud in spirit. Do not be quick in spirit to be angry or vexed, for anger and vexation *lodge* in the bosom of fools" (Ecclesiastes 7:8-9 AMP).

The end of resentment is always better than the beginning of it.

Resentment is a killer.

It leads to failure or disaster and takes unlawful residence in your heart. Anything that causes the heart to harden, and restricts the flow of God's love, forgiveness, and healing has the power to kill it.

Recently, there has been a discussion as to whether bitterness can become problematical enough to warrant being called a mental disorder. Many members of the American Psychiatric Association agreed emphatically, "YES."

Stephen Diamond, Ph.D. asserts:

Bitterness, which I define as a chronic and pervasive state of smoldering resentment, is one of the most destructive and toxic of human emotions...Bitterness is a prolonged, resentful feeling of disempowered and devalued victimization. Embitterment, like resentment and hostility, results from the long-term *mismanagement* of annoyance, irritation, frustration, anger or rage. Philosopher Friedrich Nietzsche noted that "Nothing consumes a man more quickly than the emotion of resentment." (Emphasis added)

When bitterness leaves a person, it must be replaced with something. The mind and heart are a residence. It must be filled with the presence of God. If you don't fill a heart—previously filled with anger and bitterness—with love and forgiveness, resentment will creep back in. If given the opportunity, Satan will always try to bring seven times the temptation to break down the door to your heart again, making your condition much worse than it was in the beginning.

Your age or position might command people to forgive you and move on, but appeals are stronger than demands. Forgiveness always requires consent. Loving appeals help restore what is unresolved, buried, or broken in our relationships. (See Philemon 1:8).

A few years back, my cousin, who is like a brother to me, was in a marriage crisis. He called and said, "Eddie, I messed up. She left. She won't return my texts or phone calls." After he told me the details of what happened, I asked him how long it had been since he had heard from her. He said, "One day. But I know she's leaving me." I asked him if she had told him that. He said, "No, but she has filed for child support."

I told him, "You can't repair anything if you are an angry mess. Tell her, 'If you feel safer filing child support papers, I understand.'" He then asked, "Eddie, can you call her?" I said, "No, I'm not doing that. God is teaching us, as men, how to cope better in crisis. How to get our mind out of the gutter—thinking the worst—and put it on Jesus. This will be a walk, not a sprint. Be patient."

I sent both of them some resources from the National Institute of Marriage, which were instrumental in saving my marriage. The next day, my cousin's wife called to tell me that she was going to see him and that they would be working on their marriage. When I talked to him later, I reminded him, "When you thought it was over; when you thought the marriage was dead, God was working behind the scenes in your wife to forgive you."

Anger is deadly. It breeds in assumption. It is a giant that tries to kill everything you love.

We know through history that Moses was a furious man. He killed an Egyptian and buried him in the sand. He broke the tablet with the Ten Commandments inscribed on them. He struck the rock furiously after the Israelites complained. Moses never really dealt with his anger. There was always a residue of it in his life. As a result, it kept him out of his best years—his dreams, and all God promised him.

What's keeping you from being your best? What's keeping you on the doorstep, but not barging through the gates of your highest dreams? What injustice are you still angry about in your past? Anger is a secondary emotion. What's the first one you are struggling with? What mismanagement of annoyance, irritation, frustration, anger, or fear has kept you in one place? When you are angry, it is because you are scared of something.

What are you afraid of?

Fear kept the Israelites out of the Promised Land. Anger kept Moses out (Numbers 20).

What's keeping you out?

Dream Killers

People will resent and oppose the dream or vision in your heart. It is a part of the process. You will go through desert seasons. Throughout Bible history, sometimes it took four to forty years to prepare for a vision or dream to come to pass. In an extreme case, God waited 100 years to send the rain Noah needed to get what he was building off the ground. Noah spent one century building something that saved only eight people. He made something with no guarantee. No recognition. No compensation. Only a promise that it would save his family and the next generation. Man mocked it, but God waited for him.

When people doubt or lose faith in you, do you still pursue the call of God on your life? People will either love your vision or hate it. Be prepared for both. The world is hard on dreams. They are stubborn. Jealous. Cynical. Critical, but also constructive. The Girgashite will try to drown you in worry about things you or people cannot see.

Often, we cannot see what God is doing in our lives. His hand seems invisible. Here, giants try to convince us not to come boldly. But since the beginning of time, it has been proven that when we come boldly, we see God. When we cower and hide, we don't.

The writer of Hebrews 4:16 challenges us with this: "Let us then fearlessly and confidently and boldly draw near to the throne of grace (the throne of God's unmerited favor to us sinners), that we may receive mercy [for our failures] and find grace to help in good time for every need [appropriate help and well-timed help, coming just when we need it]" (AMP).

Remember this every time you feel you aren't good enough—every time you think you don't deserve a shot, your family, or another chance in marriage. God provides mercy for failures. Mercy for your greatest sin. Mercy when you've gotten yourself fired. Mercy when you've lost every-thing. Mercy when you've tried to take your life. Mercy when bad eating habits cost you your health. Mercy. God gives us the second chance we do not deserve.

In my 20's, I spent time in church on weekdays and in clubs on weekends. I was not perfect. I'm still not. I am flawed. I have failed God repeatedly. I am a work in prog-ress. But I am not a mistake. I am not a waste. I am not a hopeless disgrace. I am what God created. I am where I need to be. God has a purpose for where he has placed me. He has a purpose for you as well. He is building something great and magnificent from the waste places of our lives.

Jesus went to the cross for our forgiveness and redemption—to see us saved, healed, restored, delivered, set free, and whole—not deficient and condemned. But giants hold our best life hostage. Satan is infuriated with the thought of us becoming all God wants us to be. He hits us over the head with a hammer and says, "Look at what you did. Look at what they did to you. Look at your parenting. Your credit. Your life. Your work history. Your career or ministry. You did this. Something is wrong with you."

Something is wrong with all of us.

We all have to work through things in life. But we are called to do it with God. To walk with Him. Pray with Him. Preach with Him. Live fearlessly through Him. Grow with Him and create new things out of nothing. We fear hell but will not fear death. Because Jesus has slain that giant. But while facing present circumstances, we must ask ourselves, "What is God trying to make me? How can my life glorify Him in this mess?" Don't spend life believing for change, but not becoming the change you want to see.

Jesus is the blueprint of all God is. He wants to express Himself through us. In John 10:10, He said, "The thief comes only to steal and kill and destroy; I have come that they may have life, and have it to the full" (NIV).

Men will let us down, but God's love is unfailing. Unceasing. As we make redemptive decisions in our lives, He is constantly releasing more of Himself to us.

As we receive more of Him, He consumes more of us. He releases more power. Power to save. Power to live righteously. Power to love. Power to keep our promises. Power to forgive. Power to dream and do the impossible. To be unshakeable giant killers.

You Deserve to Live a Full Life

I was recently onsite at a hospital doing some consulting and training. While visiting a manager, I used her restroom and on her mirror were different colored post-it notes that said, "Create the highest, grandest vision possible for your life, because you become what you believe. Remember, you are incredible. You are smart. You are kind. You matter. You are important. You have value."

I was so inspired, I stayed to read all of them. The manager shared with me that her employee, who put the notes there recently, lost her teenage daughter to suicide. Her daughter was a beautiful cheerleader, 4.0 student with a boyfriend, but because she wouldn't sleep around, her friends begin to talk about her. They called her a lesbian. They shamed, mocked, and ridiculed her for her values—because she was different. As a result, she became isolated, lonely, and depressed. One day, she was going to a sleepover at a friend's house, and the mom questioned, "Why are you going to their house, didn't you fall out with them? Aren't these the girls who started talking about you?" The daughter replied, "Yes, mom, but they are over that now."

The mom, following her intuition, called to share her concerns with the mother of the girl the daughter was going to visit. That mother spoke to her daughter, who later admitted they had invited the girl over and planned to have several guys rape her. Eventually, her boyfriend broke up with her and this beautiful sixteen-year-old girl took her own life.

The world can be cruel. People in life will hate you for no reason (John 15:18-20). But in an unbelieving world that hates you, we have a believing Jesus who loves us. He makes life worth living. In spite of your losses, He can still use you.

I love this mom. She has a lifelong mission—not to let a single day pass without posting notes telling people, "Life is tough, darling, but so are you." "You are stronger than you believe." "I believe in you even when you don't believe in yourself." "Be somebody who makes everybody feel like somebody." "Practice like you've never won. Perform like you've never lost."

Slaying Generational Giants

Have you ever given everything you have to people, and it's *still* not good enough?

Moses felt like that. He felt unappreciated by people and wanted to die because of their rejection.

Moses heard all the families standing in the doorways of their tents whining, and the Lord became extremely angry. Moses was also very aggravated.

And Moses said to the Lord, "Why are you treating me, your servant, so harshly? Have mercy on me! What did I do to deserve the burden of all these people? Did I give birth to them? Did I bring them into the world? Why did you tell me to carry them in my arms like a mother carries a nursing baby? How can I carry them to the land you swore to give their ancestors? Where am I supposed to get meat for all these people? They keep whining to me, saying, 'Give us meat to eat!' I can't carry all these people by myself! The load is far too heavy! If this is how you intend to treat me, just go ahead and kill me. Do me a favor and spare me this misery. (Numbers 11:10-15 NLT)

God had just supernaturally provided for His people to eat in the desert. Yet they are dissatisfied and discontent. They want more. And their ingratitude drives Moses to the point of suicide, as he cries to God, "If this is the best people can repay me for what I have done for them, kill me. I don't want to live anymore."

As giant killers, we carry the weight of people (*e.g.*, families, children, significant others, businesses) on our shoulders. But God understands when we get tired. He has a solution to our pain, hope for our hurt, and a plan for our future. So don't die prematurely.

Later, the Lord said to Moses, "Gather before me seventy men who are recognized as elders and leaders of Israel. Bring them to the Tabernacle to stand there *with you.* I will come down and talk to you there. I will take some of the Spirit that is upon you, and I will put the Spirit upon them also. They will bear the burden of the people along *with you, so you will not have to carry it alone* (v. 16-17 emphasis added).

God takes what is on us and puts it on other people. He will send you to gather reputable leaders in your inner circle (*e.g.*, counselors, pastors, elders) to help you carry your frustrations, anger, and resentments to the cross. Because the worst thing you can do is walk alone.

If you make straight paths for your feet to walk in the right direction and face your giants, God can cure what is lame and out of joint in your life. But you must make firm, smooth, straight paths for your feet—cutting off old ways, familiar rituals, or thought patterns (Hebrews 12:11-13).

You don't have to make the same mistakes your parents made. You don't have to perpetuate generational sin patterns in your bloodline. You don't have to do the same things your father did. You can be what God intended through disciplined, powerful, and redemptive decisions. You can ensure the success and not the suicide of your dreams. At twenty-three years and running, my wife and I currently hold the record of the longest marriage in my family. I want our kids to break our record. I want to inspire them to get and stay married—to defeat the giant of dissatisfaction and divorce.

I once heard T.D. Jakes quote King Solomon, saying, "A good man leaves an inheritance to his children's children. God has set it up that you will not know the kind of man I am until you see my children's children—how my direct parenting influenced theirs." This principle challenges us to the core of what we leave our children.

Don't Give Your Children Your Giants

In Genesis 4:3-7, Adam's son Cain is attacked by the same giant of dissatisfaction that Adam had fallen to.

> In the course of time Cain brought some of the fruits of the soil as an offering to the Lord. And Abel also brought an offering—fat portions from some of the firstborn of his flock. The Lord looked with favor on Abel and his offering, but on Cain and his offering he did not look with favor. So Cain was very angry, and his face was downcast. Then the Lord said to Cain, "Why are you angry? Why is your face downcast? If you do what is right, will you not be accepted? But if you do not do what is right, sin is crouching at your door; it desires to have you, but you must rule over it. (NIV)

Here, Cain is dealing with the shame of being rejected. He brings an offering with his brother, but while Abel's gift is accepted, his is not. Immediately, he feels worthless, unloved, and rejected.

That's the message of shame.

Cain's anger and dissatisfaction desires to have him. Likewise, sin crouches at our door in many forms:

- Anger
- Bitterness
- Lust
- Pride
- Greed
- Ingratitude, etc.

But God's response to Cain's dissatisfaction was simple. Change the seed you are sowing. If you don't like the harvest you received in life, plant a different seed. You change your harvest with your seed.

Instead, Cain attacked what was the trigger—the constant reminder of his failure in life. First, he "acted in" by being angry. Smoldering with resentment. Not talking to his brother. Trying to transfer all the rejection, insignificance, and failure he felt to Abel. Then he "acted out" by attacking. "Now Cain said to his brother Abel, 'Let's go out to the field.' While they were in the field, Cain attacked his brother Abel and killed him. Then the Lord said to Cain, 'Where is your brother Abel?'" (Genesis 4:8-9 NIV).

Notice, in Genesis 3:9, God asked a similar question to Cain's father Adam after he sinned. The sins of our father will often have macro results on us. Eventually, God cursed the area of life which Cain refused to change.

Sin and shame always hide behind something. It crouches to remain hidden, bringing sudden destruction in our lives. But Jesus loved and lived a perfect life to give His perfect record to us—to give us a blood transfusion of His life, His thoughts, His ways in place of ours.

We have a responsibility to teach our children lessons from our wisdom gained—to share wins and losses. God never intended us to pass bad inheritances to the next generation. We have a good inheritance from Jesus. He put the bad family history of humanity on the cross and killed it.

Give Him yours.

CHAPTER 5

THE GIANT OF UNFORGIVENESS

Amorites: Mountain people. Renowned. Obsession with earthly fame, glory, and dictatorship.

Have you ever wanted someone to pay for what they did to you? Been traumatized by unforgiveness? An unjustifiable wrong? A parent hurt you. A boyfriend broke up with you. A spouse cheated. A sibling tried to steal your parent's inheritance. A co-worker took credit for your work. A boss fired you. A pastor divided the church. A friend betrayed you. A family member or stranger abused you. A criminal killed someone you loved.

Jonah was a man who ran from the call of God. He didn't want Nineveh saved or forgiven. Infuriated with their outrageously sinful lifestyles, he wanted them to die. Eventually, he asked God, "Just kill me now, Lord! I'd rather be dead than alive if what I predicted will not happen" (Jonah 4:3 NLT).

Jonah was more concerned about his reputation as a prophet than God's reputation as a healer.

Nineveh, the capital of Assyria, was a cruel and historical nemesis of Israel and Judah. Founded by Nimrod, great-grandson of Noah (Genesis 10:6–12), the Ninevites had pillaged the Jews. They raped their women and killed their people. Jonah could not excuse and forgive their actions. Thus, the story of Jonah is more than a story about a fish. It is a story about human pride and anger.

Jonah wanted Nineveh to pay for what they did. People will do things that make your heart feel that way. They will test your forgiveness, grace, and humility. But God never gives up on us. We are called to forgive. The Prophet Samuel once wrote: "You rescue the humble, but your eyes watch the proud and humiliate them" (2 Samuel 22:28 NLT).

The Israelites had to confront the Amorite giant next. Amorites were renowned giants that lived in the mountains. According to the website *Shamah Elim*:

"Amorite" means, "mountain people; renowned." Since mountains refer to tall and impressive land masses that dominate over valleys, we can infer that the Amorite spirit is a spirit of self-exaltation. The word for Amorite in Hebrew comes from another Hebrew word, *amar*, which means, "to utter, to say"; this implies that people with Amorite spirits are people who want their name uttered or mentioned. Amorites are fame-seekers, seekers of human glory and greatness.

Sometimes, we seek the fame of our name, rank, or title at the expense of forgiveness. We long to hear the words, "You were right," in disagreements. I have struggled with this Amorite giant in the past. When I did not get my way or felt disrespected, or perhaps inadequate, by something my wife said, I engaged in a "silent war" with her, withdrawing my presence. I was "acting in" like Absalom, trying to transfer everything I feel (*e.g.*, rejection, isolation, unloved) to her. I wanted her to utter my name and apologize first. After all, she did it. Like Adam in the Garden of Eden, I shifted blame. She insulted me first. She brought up what I deemed a hysterical fear or something that happened in the past.

Have you ever been there before? Have you ever walked into a room and knew the other person was upset, even though they didn't say a word? Have you ever given someone the silent treatment that lasted days, weeks, years, and eventually decades?

God wants to give you more than the earthly fame of being right—hearing your name. More than your dream. More than material things. He wants to cut off the head of your giant. He wants your pride. To take away the distress you've been carrying. That word "distress" means "1. To pain; to greatly afflict the body or the mind with anguish; 2. To harass; to oppress with calamity; to make miserable" (KJV Dictionary).

One of my favorite heroes of forgiveness in the Bible is Joseph. Joseph was the favorite son of his father Israel, who gave him a robe of many colors. He was a dreamer.

One day, Joseph shared his dreams with his brothers, and they hated him even more. His brothers thought the only way to stop his destiny was to kill him. They ended up selling him into slavery. Even in this most bitter betrayal—stripped of his coat of many colors, thrown into a well, and sold out by his own siblings—we can see the hand of God, setting the stage for Joseph to rule and provide for his family in Egypt.

Joseph not only provided for them during famine, he saved them from their own distresses—their guilt and shame. The biblical account of this family's reconciliation is found in Genesis 45.

"Please, come closer," he said to them. So they came closer. And he said again, "I am Joseph, your brother, whom you sold into slavery in Egypt. But don't be upset, and don't be angry with yourselves for selling me to this place. It was God who sent me here ahead of you to preserve your lives. This famine that has ravaged the land for two years will last five more years, and there will be neither plowing nor harvesting. God has sent me ahead of you to keep you and your families alive and to preserve many survivors. So it was God who sent me here, not you! And he is the one who made me an adviser to Pharaoh—the manager of his entire palace and the governor of all Egypt." (v. 4-8 NLT)

The Black Box

When Joseph's brothers came to him, he pardoned them. The transformation God began in Joseph, while in slavery and prison to forgive their betrayal, was still at work. Even when he had an opportunity to pay them back, he refused to retaliate. Grudges are fatal to your dreams. Sometimes when people wrong us, we want them to be as captive to the memory of the event as we are. We want them to be our slaves. To do whatever we want. Whatever we need when a "trigger" reminds us of the injustice. The truth is, it still hurts like it was yesterday.

But God does not intend for us to live with powerless ghosts of our past. The prophet Isaiah wrote a stirring declaration: "O Lord, our God, other masters besides You have ruled over us, but we will acknowledge and mention Your name only. They [the former tyrant masters] are dead, they shall not live and reappear; *they are powerless ghosts*, they shall not rise and come back. Therefore, You have visited and made an end of them and caused every memory of them *[every trace of their supremacy] to perish*" (Isaiah 26:13 AMP).

God wants to put an end to every memory, every trace, and ghost of our tormenting past. He wants them never to reappear in our lives again. But our heart is a tricky thing. It is sensitive. It makes us think we're over something, then suddenly, just like that, it remembers. A therapist at the National Institute of Marriage, once said to me, "Our hearts are like black boxes in airplanes."

Black boxes help investigators determine what happened in an airplane disaster by recording the good and bad—normal and abnormal events. Even if the airliner crashes at sea and all passengers are lost, this little black box has the durability and design to survive. The federal government will send divers past floating debris and victims to find this small black box to see what went wrong.

Why?

Because it remembers both the good and the bad. It remembers everything from, "Thank you for choosing ABC Airlines," to the worst news imaginable, "There is smoke in the engine! Mayday! Mayday!" In this little black box, every event, every detail is recorded.

That's our heart.

It remembers. Every celebration. Every achievement. Every milestone. Every heartbreak. Every betrayal. Every rejection, abuse, and injustice. It remembers what we want to forget. It knows no time. That's how a fifty-year old man, abandoned by his father at five, can still painfully react to rejection by his dad as an adult. That's how a woman, molested at nine, still has problems trusting in relationships at forty-nine. Because this heart remembers things as if it happened yesterday.

Out of this heart—filled with all kinds of hurts, insecurities, false opinions, conflicts, criticisms, and negative thoughts—our mouth speaks—no matter where we go. Just as age will not improve a diagnosis left untreated, the heart does not change with time. Geographies don't erase it. Birthdays don't change it. A new car or spouse won't placate it.

Kenny Bryant, my therapist at the National Institute of Marriage once said, "60-70% of the way we put things in our heart is determined by age 5-7. As children, we are great observers instead of thinkers."

When I was young, I saw my mom do everything without my father around. She had to fight on her own. Fight to make a living. Fight as a female evangelist in a male-dominated ministry. Fight my family from taking me to the People's Temple. Fight Jim Jones. Fight to protect me. The fighting made her very strong and independent, but also distrusting of people. Always suspicious. As a child observer, it taught me not to trust anyone. If I wanted something done right, I would have to do it myself.

I left home at nineteen after a heated argument with my mom, when she said, "You still need a woman to take care of you." I had just finished a business school course and was working in telemarketing. So, I left to show my mom I could do more with my life. To start a career. Start a business. I wanted to prove, after all the years she took care of me, by herself, that I could take care of myself and perhaps her one day. I wanted to make her proud. She had done enough.

The first three days, I lived in my car in South Central Los Angeles. I was terrified. Random people came and knocked on my window throughout the night. I eventually got my first apartment on the second floor above an auto repair shop. The studio smelled like gasoline and oil. I got a roommate, but it was short-lived. He spent his rent on drugs, so I moved out. I found another roommate, but he was sleeping with someone else's girlfriend. I was up all night either because her boyfriend was banging on the door, or they were having loud sex in the bedroom next to me. Again, I moved out.

These experiences were the catalyst that fueled my independence and distrust of people. It even affected my marriage. I didn't trust my wife initially when we married. My heart had not changed all those years. I was still trying to prove that I could take care of myself without anyone's help. That I didn't need anyone to succeed—not even her.

Sometimes, we are still trying to prove people, from our past, wrong. Something happened that broke us, and we are no longer reacting to what people do. We are reacting to our fears, our past hurts, or triggers that remind us of what happened. We are responding to someone in our past when speaking to someone in our present.

The Wrong Well

In John 4, when Jesus asked the Samaritan woman for a drink, she replied, "You are a Jew, and I am a Samaritan woman. Why are you asking me for a drink?" The woman was surprised, because Jews refused to have anything to do with Samaritans. She was speaking of a hurt or inequality in her past or of a person in her present. But in Jn 4:13-18, Jesus replied,

"Anyone who drinks this water will soon become thirsty again. But those who drink the water I give will never be thirsty again. It becomes a fresh, bubbling spring within them, giving them eternal life." "Please, sir," the woman said, "give me this water! Then I'll never be thirsty again, and I won't have to come here to get water." "Go and get your husband," Jesus told her. "I don't have a husband," the woman replied. Jesus said, "You're right! You don't have a husband—for you have had five husbands, and you aren't even married to the man you're living with now." (NLT)

Jesus tells the woman at the well, she has been married five times to the wrong person. Five times to the wrong desires. Five times to the wrong well. The wrong entertainment. The wrong addiction or high. The wrong excuses.

She is thirsty and looking for something—anything that will satisfy the desert in her life, so Jesus offers her a drink. Sadly, we can spend our entire lives married to the wrong thing, drawing from the well of men or humanity.

Married to our carnal senses:

- What we see.
- What we hear.
- What we touch.
- What we taste.
- What we smell.

Married to fear. A job. A pandemic. An ideal. A belief system. A privilege or bias. An offense. A victim mentality. A wrong way of doing things.

But just because you have watered your life from the same place your ancestors have, doesn't mean you have to keep drawing from there.

The woman at the well was on her sixth man. She was angry and defensive, because carnal emotions will never satisfy us. When relationships fail repeatedly, we often become detached. Unmarried. Unhappy. Unwilling to give anything (or anyone) a chance to hurt us again.

Here in John 4, Jesus crossed tense racial and gender divides to have a conversation with a distrusting and hurting woman. After her encounter and revelation with Him, her cycle of bad marriages ended. Jesus was the seventh and last man in her life (seven is the number of completion). He was the well and living water she had been looking for, the marriage she'd always hoped and dreamed of. This woman went from being a well drawer to a city evangelist.

Likewise, when we encounter Jesus, He will change our life. Change our heart. Change our choices. Change our reputation.

God changes lifestyles and occupations for a living.

He makes incomplete lives whole. Broken, deficient, and oppressed lives matter. Unlike our previous loves, He never breaks our heart, runs out on us, or leaves us thirsty. He fills us with endless joy, life, and streams of living water.

What well are you drinking from today?

Jesus came to save you from that watering place. The bad marriage you are in. The destructive cycle you've repeated. The inequity you've experienced. He comes to where we are. When we are thirsty, dissatisfied, and discontent.

In John 4:12, the Samaritan woman was skeptical and said to Jesus, "Do you think you're greater than our ancestor Jacob, who gave us this well? How can you offer better water than he and his sons and his animals enjoyed?"

But Jesus is greater than our family tree, traditions, patterns, and ways. He will give us something better than what our ancestors drank from in life. When He fills us, out of the abundance of our heart, our mouth speaks—drawing families, neighborhoods, cities, and industries to Him.

God Restores Hearts

We must ask God to retrain and rewire our heart. From the heart, powerful words that change times and seasons can be released. But sometimes this black box—this heart—is lost and buried without a signal to find it. God promised to take our hearts of stone and make them hearts of flesh (Ezekiel 36:26). He can take our distress, shame, fear, and guilt away if we bring them to Him.

Jesus came to give us a clear conscience from our giants. The things we have done in our past. The people we have hurt. The people who hurt us. The betrayal and bitterness we harbor. He came to restore our hearts and broken lives.

In Hebrews 9:10, the Greek word *diothosis* is used to define restoration as "to set things right," or "to snap a broken bone back into place." Restoring doesn't mean going back to what was. When God restores something, He makes it better than new. By faith and through God's healing process, somehow, someway, He does this super-naturally in us, so that we can do it for others. Sometimes in a home restoration, you gut everything over and start new, so when you walk into it, it is unrecognizable.

God snaps broken and dislocated lives back into place.

Job 8:5-7 says, "But if you pray to God and seek the favor of the Almighty, and if you are pure and live with integrity, he will surely rise up and restore your happy home. And though you started with little, you will end with much" (NLT).

How can we tell if our hearts are being restored? Our mouth changes. Over time, we don't sound the same in conflict. We showcase who God is making us. We have more wins, than losses. We believe in restoration. When things don't go our way, we don't react immediately with anger. We don't talk about people behind their backs. We don't remind them of what they have done in the past or shut them down with our words. We snap less at people. We are not bitter. We are beautiful. A masterpiece. Because change is present.

That's what happened to Joseph. He went from telling Pharaoh's officials he was forcibly kidnapped from home and didn't deserve to be in prison (Genesis 40), to telling his brothers, "It was not you who sent me here, but God"

(Genesis 45). Joseph's heart was healed from the distress and betrayal inflicted by his brothers.

Who else was distressed in Joseph's life?

His brothers. "Joseph's brothers said to one another, 'Surely, we are being punished because of our brother. We saw how distressed he was when he pleaded with us for his life, but we would not listen; that's why this distress has come on us'" (Genesis 42:21 NIV). Joseph's brothers felt distressed because of something they did in the past.

Ever felt like that? Like God is allowing some pain in your life, because of a mistake in the past—some pain or sin you caused? I have news for you. God is not in heaven with a baseball bat looking for ways to get back at us. Jesus came to save the world, not condemn it. He came to save our marriages. Save our children. Save our conscience. And His grace is all we need. It is sufficient for you and me. When we come to Him, His divine purpose is to make us whole. Not broken. Not deficient. Not defeated. Not dependent on man. Not fearful. Not sick. Not depressed. Not destitute. Not hopeless. Not inadequate or incomplete.

When we come to Him, He gives us what we do not deserve. He takes away all the distress, guilt, punishment, and shame we have carried these years.

Joseph's father was also distressed. Imagine being one of Jacob's sons when they returned from Egypt, where Joseph had told his men to put his brothers' payments back in their sacks of grain. Imagine the scene when they got back to Jacob:

As they emptied out their sacks, there in each man's sack was the bag of money he had paid for the grain! The brothers and their father were terrified when they saw the bags of money. Jacob exclaimed, "You are robbing me of my children! Joseph is gone! Simeon is gone! And now you want to take Benjamin, too. Everything is going against me!" Then Reuben said to his father,"You may kill my two sons if I don't bring Benjamin back to you. I'll be responsible for him, and I promise to bring him back." But Jacob replied, "My son will not go down with you. His brother Joseph is dead, and he is all I have left. If anything should happen to him on your journey, you would send this grieving, white-haired man to his grave." (Genesis 42:35-38 NLT)

Jacob was distressed, living a life of sorrow. In Genesis 37, Jacob was the one who told Joseph to go see about his brothers when he disappeared. Jacob's sons had stripped, beaten, and sold Joseph into slavery, but reported to their father that he had been eaten by a wild animal. Jacob lived with this guilt for years. But Joseph, a type of Christ, had been sent ahead of them. He had been promoted by the system that enslaved him—as a father to Pharaoh (Genesis 45:8). With a name above all in Egypt, he had the position and power to free his family from all those years of regret and blame.

Maybe you feel like Joseph's brothers and father. You feel responsible for what you did in the past. Responsible for what happened to your lost children. Weighed down with guilt over their decisions. Struggling over what's in the rearview mirror of your past. Responsible for someone who died prematurely. Maybe you feel you were at fault, that you could have done more to save them, or worse, it should have been you.

Jesus came to save us from that thinking. From every trouble. Every distress. Every blame. Every heartache. The pride of thinking we were in control, and he was not. The Amorite giant glories in self. But God said if you come to me, "I will give you a new heart, a new spirit to hear me—a heart sensitive and responsive to my touch and voice, not your pain" (See Ezekiel 11:19). When we come into the presence of God, He gives us something that won't hurt anymore. A peace that transcends all human understanding. Joy, unspeakable joy. An everlasting love that conquers all—believes all and is stronger than what tried to kill it.

It's Never Too Late

My pastor told us a story some years ago about a young girl in South Africa who died and went to heaven. She was a problem child who gave her parents a lot of grief. One day, her parents took her to the hospital where she became unconscious and suddenly died. The physicians frantically tried to resuscitate her. After five minutes, she came back to life and shared how she went to heaven and stepped into the presence of God. She said heaven was the most beautiful place she had ever seen. Jesus had the most beautiful face she had ever witnessed before. When Jesus asked her, "Do you want to stay?" She replied, "Yes, Jesus, I want to stay." Then Jesus took his hand and rolled back the clouds like a curtain. From there, in heaven, she saw the doctors over her lifeless body, trying to bring her back. She saw an adjacent room where her mother and father were crying uncontrollably, and her little brother was playing with a toy truck. Then she said to Jesus, "Jesus, I must go back." He looked at her and said, "Tell my people I'm coming soon, and I will see you soon." After she came back to life, she testified in many churches about her experience in the presence of God. She lived a life radically changed by her encounter with Jesus. After three years of preaching the gospel, she went to a doctor's visit one day. He administered the wrong shot to her, and she died instantly. Everyone around her was stunned. As they began to watch video of her testimony, they kept stopping and rewinding to the place where Jesus said, "Tell my people I'm coming soon, *and I will see you soon.*" Her time was limited on earth to live a life changed by the presence of God.

So is ours.

Don't wait until you are old to live right for God—to fulfill your call or dream. As King Solomon wrote,

Don't let the excitement of youth cause you to forget your Creator. Honor him in your youth before you grow old and say, 'Life is not pleasant anymore.' Remember him before the light of the sun, moon, and stars is dim to your old eyes, and rain clouds continually darken your sky. Remember him before your legs—the guards of your house—start to tremble; and before your shoulders—the strong men—stoop. Remember him before your teeth— your few remaining servants—stop grinding; and before your eyes—the women looking through the windows—see dimly. Remember him before the door to life's opportunities is closed and the sound of work fades...Remember him before you near the grave, your everlasting home, when the mourners will weep at your funeral. (Ecclesiastics 12:1-5 NLT)

Don't wait until your strength is dried up. Until doors close. Until giants become bigger or produce fear. Don't waste your best years being afraid. Being angry. Don't let the passion or dream die. Do it while you are fearless. Do it while you feel brave. Live for Him while you have vigor and strength. Sometimes your latter years are the greatest years of your life.

Jesus promised, "He will not crush the weakest reed, or put out a flickering candle. Finally, he will cause justice to be victorious. And his name will be the hope of all the world" (Matthew 12:20-21 NLT).

When justice seems lost—when we are bruised and weakened by failure or defeat, barely flickering with hope in that dead-end job or relationship, we have a promise that Jesus will not leave us broken. He will not put us out. We will win. He will heal and restore us. Our judge will redeem us from pain, bitterness, loss, and distress.

God promised through the Prophet Joel, "I will give you back what you lost to the swarming locusts, the hopping locusts, the stripping locusts, and the cutting locusts. It was I who sent this great destroying army against you. Once again you will have all the food you want, and you will praise the Lord your God, who does these miracles for you. Never again will my people be disgraced" (Joel 2:25-26 NLT).

Charles Spurgeon once preached:

It will strike you at once that the locusts did not eat the years: the locusts ate the fruits of the year's labor (the harvests of the fields); so that the meaning of the restoration of the years must be the restoration of those fruits and of those harvests which the locusts consumed. You cannot have your time back; but there is a strange and wonderful way in which God can give back to you the wasted blessings, the unripened fruits of years over which you mourned. The fruits of wasted years may still be yours. It is a pity that they should have been locust-eaten by your folly and negligence; but if they have been so, do not be hopeless concerning them. 'All things are possible for him who believes.' There is a power which is beyond all things, and can work great marvels. Who can make the all-devouring locust restore his prey? No man, by wisdom or power, can recover what has been utterly destroyed. Only God can do for you what seems impossible; and here is the promise of his grace: 'I will restore to you the years that the locust has eaten.' (*A Sermon Delivered on Lord's Day Evening*, May 30, 1886)

After our worst season. Our worst chastisement. Our worst defeat. After all the years we lost and fell behind. The years we did not finish the degree. Finish the book. Finish the project. God still promises an outpouring of restoration. He promised, "I can restore the years. I'll give them back to you!"

Double for our shame. Double for the years stolen by bad decisions or resentment towards others. We cannot get back our time, our labor, the seeds we've sown, or the years we've sown them in. But God can restore the seemingly wasted efforts. The rewards and fruit you lost. The money they should have paid you for your service. The position awarded to someone else. The church or business someone else was asked to lead. The harvest of wasted years is yours.

We All Have Blind Spots

Blind spots are areas of our lives we can't see—fast approaching to cause a collision. We must deal with the areas we are purposefully blind to—that we refuse to change.

Blind spots can kill us.

What you don't acknowledge in your rear-view mirror can collide with you. But Jesus came to reveal anything that can kill, steal, and destroy in your life. He came to give life, not death. To save, not destroy. He simply asks us—flaws and all—to come to Him.

> "Turn to me now," says the Lord, "while there is time. Give me your hearts. Come with fasting, weeping, and mourning. Don't tear your clothing in your grief, but tear your hearts instead." Return to the Lord your God, for He is merciful and compassionate, slow to get angry and filled with unfailing love. He is eager to relent and *not punish*. Who knows? Perhaps he will give you a reprieve, sending you a blessing instead of this curse. (Joel 2:12-14 NLT)

There is a blessing behind our worst season and diagnosis. God left the blessing behind for us to serve Him with fruit, not failure. To be powerful, not pitiful. To be champions, not cowards.

We choose.

CHAPTER 6

THE GIANT OF ADDICTION

Canaanites: Lowlands people. Addictions. Perversions. A desire to please others with base values.

As you read through the giants we face in this book, which one is taunting you in your life, authority, and dreams? How many wins and losses do you have in your daily battles? Is your progress in living through Jesus—your giant killer—all you dreamed it would be? Are you content where you are?

You will stay in the place of dissatisfaction until you deal with addictions in your life. You can face this giant of addiction, in one or more of these areas:

- Sex
- Food
- Pornography
- Video games
- Exercising

- Working
- Shopping
- Alcohol
- Opioids
- Prescription Drugs
- Gambling
- Stealing
- Intermittent explosive disorder; *i.e.*, compulsive aggressive and assaultive acts (*HealthyPlace.com*)

The apostle Paul exhorted the church in Ephesus: "Let there be no sexual immorality, impurity, or greed among you. Such sins have no place among God's people. Obscene stories, foolish talk, and coarse jokes—these are not for you. Instead, let there be thankfulness to God. You can be sure that no immoral, impure, or greedy person will inherit the Kingdom of Christ and of God. For a greedy person is an idolater, worshiping the things of this world" (Ephesians 5:3-5 NLT). Paul admonishes us to live our life above the reproach of accusation of sin: sexual addictions, greed (addiction to money), or other impurities listed above. Any of these addictions are idolatry.

On the eve before a decision to sign a publishing deal for *Be A Giant Killer*, my wife and I were arguing. She was upstairs. I was downstairs. Every movie channel was showing explicit movies. Satan was at work that day, but by God's grace, I resisted the temptation. I passed by the bad movies and gained a win.

Whatever is keeping you from winning—being effective, advancing, and increasing in life—must be dealt with in order to rise to the next one. Nations cannot come to you. True wealth cannot come to you. Favor and influence cannot come until certain things—hindrances—leave your life.

Temptation is a fire fueled by decisions. We don't fall into it overnight. Minor decisions become macro results. We give in. We get angry. We vent. We let something into our lives through our eyes or actions.

Here is the good news: God uses us while He changes us.

We have all sinned and fallen short of the glory of God. We all need a savior. A new DNA. New heart. New eyes. New desires. Jesus supplied these in human form when He was nailed to the cross. When we accept Him into our lives, and He transforms us by the renewing of our mind, we change. We get better. We gain more wins than losses in certain areas.

But just like we cannot violate a company rule or policy repeatedly and say to our employer, "Well everyone makes mistakes," God's grace was not given to us so sin could abound, but so the power of a new life and giant killer could arise.

Two Natures

Two natures are at war within us: A giant killer and a Goliath. According to *Behindthename.com*, the Hebrew word for Goliath is *Golyat*, possibly derived from *galah*, and means "to uncover, or reveal."

The giant in our life exposes what is in us. What's in our heart will eventually be revealed. Whichever nature we feed will grow stronger and overpower the other.

The apostle Paul wrote to the Galatians, "Don't be misled—you cannot mock the justice of God. You will always harvest what you plant. Those who live only to satisfy their own sinful nature will harvest decay and death from that sinful nature. But those who live to please the Spirit will harvest everlasting life from the Spirit. So, let's not get tired of doing what is good. At just the right time we will reap a harvest of blessing if we don't give up" (Galatians 6:7-9 NLT).

This is the high privilege of a giant killer. Each one's life reveals what he has asked for and sown. The Book of Job introduces Job, a blameless man of complete integrity. There was no one like him. Job was extremely successful, the richest person in his area. He feared God and stayed away from evil (Job 1:1-3 NLT). Likewise, we have to stay away from our addictions. We can't just pray them away. Whatever giant we are living in proximity to will try to kill us.

Matthew Henry's Commentary says this about Job 31:1-9:

> The lusts of the flesh, and the love of the world, are the two fatal rocks on which multitudes split; against these Job protests he was always careful to

106

stand upon his guard against the lusts of the flesh. He not only kept himself clear from adultery, from defiling his neighbors' wives (v. 9), but from all lewdness with any women whatsoever. He kept no concubine, no mistress, but was inviolably faithful to the marriage bed, *though his wife* was none of *the wisest, best, or kindest.*

The writer of the book of Job wrote, "Uncontrolled or unconquered areas of our flesh are destructive fires that (left unchecked) can consume all your life's increase" (Job 31:11-12 AMP).

As giant killers, we must constantly pursue discipline, no matter what people do in our lives. If we are ill-disciplined—if we cannot control our tongue, eyes, thoughts, flesh, deeds, or actions—or always blame others for what we do, then we have no right to authority or dominion. The devil didn't make you do it. *You did it.* He may have influenced us, but God always provides a way of escape.

In *The Willpower Instinct: How Self-Control Works, Why it Matters, and What You Can Do to Get More of It,* Kelly McGonigal asserts:

People who have better control of their attention, emotions, and actions are better off almost any way you look at it. They are happier and healthier. Their relationships are more satisfying and last longer. They make more money and go further in their careers. They are better able to manage stress, deal with conflict, and overcome adversity. They even live longer. When pit against other virtues, willpower comes out on top. Self-control is a better predictor of academic success than intelligence… a stronger determinant of effective leadership than charisma…. and more important for marital bliss than empathy…

Don't forfeit your dreams and goals because you lack self-control. We must control our life before we control our destiny. We must discipline our mind and body in order to reach the finish line.

King Solomon wrote, "Better to be patient than powerful; better to have self-control than to conquer a city" (Proverbs 16:32 NLT).

We must be disciples (disciplined ones) with habits that form wins and championships, not defeat and disqualifications.

Twins

The way of escape is through new birth. This is the account of the family of Isaac, the son of Abraham:

> When Isaac was forty years old, he married Rebekah, the daughter of Bethuel the Aramean from Paddan-aram and the sister of Laban the Aramean. Isaac pleaded with the Lord on behalf of his wife, because she was unable to have children. The Lord answered Isaac's prayer, and Rebekah

became pregnant with twins. But the two children struggled with each other in her womb. So she went to ask the Lord about it. "Why is this happening to me?" she asked. And the Lord told her, "The sons in your womb will become two nations. From the very beginning, the two nations will be rivals. One nation will be stronger than the other; and your older son will serve your younger son." And when the time came to give birth, Rebekah discovered that she did indeed have twins. (Genesis 25:19-24 NLT)

Jacob and Esau were two babies born of the same body. One hairy. One with smooth skin. One stronger. One weaker. Twins, but different in nature.

Likewise, two natures are struggling inside of you—one greater, one anointed. The "second you" is an endangered species—a unicorn—something people, your family, your spouse, and children have never seen before. Just like the second Adam, Jesus, is greater than the first Adam, God said, the "first you" would bow to the "second you." The old you will serve the new you—the saved, sanctified, freed, healed, and wiser you. You are in a better place than you think you are. The "new you" will be the best "you."

No matter how much you have failed, the next chapter of your marriage, relationships, parenting (even adult kids), and life decisions can be better. In the book *How We Love* by Milan and Kay Yerkovich, the authors claim, "Our ability to love is shaped by our first experiences with our parents and caregivers during our early years. These early experiences leave a lasting imprint on our souls that is still observable in our adult relationships."

My wife recently told me, "It took us twenty years to do for our kids, what it took our parents more than forty years to do for us." No matter who we were when people first met us, the next time they see us, we will be different. Because God can transform the worst seasons (and decisions) of our lives into the best years of our lives.

The "first you" represents the "physically born you," which will one day die. The "second you" represents the "born-again you" which, in Christ, will live forever. That will rise again. Overcome the grave. Become president of the system that imprisoned you—a father to the Pharaohs in your industry. Part Red Seas. Bring walled cities down. Shut the mouth of lions. Walk in fire and kill Goliath.

But you must separate the "first you" from the "second you." The younger twin—the most recent "you"—must be stronger than the older version of "you." We must kill the old nature, so a new one can live. Jesus said in Matthew 6:24, "No one can serve two masters. Either you will hate the one and love the other, or you will be devoted to the one and despise the other" (NIV).

If you are going to change, why not change now? You can leave your marriage, job, school, or city, but if you don't change *you*, the result will be the same. Why have your children raised by someone else? Why waste the years of equity you have built on that job? Why run from relationship to relationship, job to job, or city to city?

The "second you" can be better.

Life Is a Journey

My pastor once said, "Dominion is a process, and authority requires discipline." Until Christ came, man had authority, but broken dominion. While influence can be given in titles by men, dominion only comes from God. After creation, God blessed Adam and Eve, telling them, "Be fruitful, multiply, and fill the earth, and subdue it [using all its vast resources in the service of God and man]; and have dominion" (Genesis 1:28 AMP).

When you have legal authority or rule over something, you have dominion. Dominion requires constant submission, right decision making, and self-correction. James wrote, "Remember, it is sin to know what you ought to do and then not do it (4:17 NLT). A title or authority is nothing without dominion.

This means we have *not* arrived. A PhD, a big church, sold-out events, a private jet, fancy car, luxury home, a successful or Fortune 500 company is not an indication of arrival. We can have authority as a home or business owner for twenty years and lose it in twenty minutes because we had no dominion. Our journey from conception to beyond the grave is a journey to an infinitely holy God. We can never say, "I have arrived." We will never know everything about God. We will never be experts on the ways, purposes, and thoughts of God. The more we know about God, the more we realize how much we don't know. The fact is we have a perspective of reality that is at best partial.

The apostle Paul taught his spiritual son Timothy: "Do not waste time arguing over godless ideas and old wives' tales. Instead, train yourself to be godly. Physical training is good, but training for godliness is much better, promising benefits in this life and in the life to come" (1 Timothy 4:7-8 NLT).

In other words, don't fall for quick fixes or gimmicks. People who offer easy solutions for difficult problems. Sexting or porn on social media for loneliness. Easy pay for hard work. Overnight wealth or success for no work. Handwritten signs at street intersections that say you can work from home and make $5-10,000 per month. As a successful entrepreneur, I guarantee you if I pay someone that kind of money per month, I will not recruit them from a freeway exit.

The Canaanite Giant

Ever heard the old adage, "You are what you eat"? Whatever is in our diet will determine our appearance in life. Our lives are the total of what we consume by study, practice, training, observation, literature, and the Word of God.

My writing mentor Leslie Stobbe recently shared a passage from 2 Timothy 4:3-4, which reminded me of why so many died in Jonestown. The apostle Paul told Timothy, "For a time is coming when people will no longer listen to sound and wholesome teaching. They will follow their own desires and will look for teachers who will tell them whatever their itching ears want to hear. They will reject the truth and chase after myths" (NLT).

We live in a fast-paced society where people have a drive-through mentality. They want the promise without the process. Promotion without pain. To avoid discipline at all costs. That is the Canaanite giant. The Canaanite condescends to low earthly, sensual passions. They are spirits behind addictions, sexual immorality, and perversions. The temptation to impurity is a constant threat to our anointing and dreams. God created marriage to help counter it, but the truth is, we need more than just a spouse. We need sexual integrity. We need it in our lives and in the people we choose to share our lives with.

Sodom and Gomorrah were Canaanite cities, where spirits of excess—fornication, pornography, and homosexuality—originated (Genesis 18:20. See also Genesis 10:19; 13:12-13). The Canaanite giant operates through emotions to shut off your godly mindset and good judgment (1 Corinthians 2:13-16).

When our calling or dream hasn't fully come to pass, Satan loves to discourage us, tempting us to make hasty decisions that disqualify us. Don't fall for that trap. Keep your highest dream, life, and calling in front of you. Don't let it fall behind you. Don't forfeit your destiny and inheritance for one meal. One night. One indulgence. One bad decision. Excess kills.

King Solomon wrote, "Do you like honey? Don't eat too much, or it will make you sick!" (Proverbs 25:16 NLT).

We have need of not only patience, but self-control. People who fall into drug addiction or alcoholism, generally are influenced by people or circumstances that scream, "Everyone is doing it. One sip, one puff won't hurt you." But five-second decisions can start a painful reign of destructive patterns in your life. If it's okay to try it now, it reinforces the decision to try it later when things are worse. Decisions qualify or disqualify us. We close doors opened by bad decisions, by opening doors to good ones. If not, our history will eventually play out in life. It will drive everything we think or do. Max De Pree once wrote, "We cannot become what we want, by remaining what we are."

Our Family Tree

It's easy to feel like a failure.

It's easy to look back at what you lost and say, "I ruined everything." But so did Adam and Eve. They had a perfect marriage, a perfect home, a perfect father, and they squandered it all.

In Genesis 3:6, we see the first deception of the flesh: "When the woman saw that the fruit of the tree was 'good for food' and pleasing to the eye, and also desirable for gaining wisdom, she took some and ate it. She also gave some to her husband, who was with her, and he ate it. Then the eyes of both of them were opened, and they realized they were naked; so they sewed fig leaves together and made coverings for themselves" (AMP).

Notice, the tree they picked from was "good for food," but not good for them. Something can be good for entertainment sales (*e.g.*, porn), but not good for you. Good for employment income (*e.g.*, erotic dancing), to take your loneliness away *(e.g.*, one-night stands), to make the pain go away (*e.g.*, addictions), to meet your immediate financial need (*e.g.*, bad loans with exorbitant interest rates), but not good for you.

For example, once a person's judgment against heavy narcotic use and drinking has been shut off, the person indulges. Soon all sober judgment and inhibition are gone. Drunkenness and bad decisions follow. When I was young, often I would drink to get my mind to shut off wise choices—to create excuses for immorality. That was the Canaanite giant. You can either harbor the Canaanite in your life or become an enabler to someone with it. If a loved one is struggling to defeat addiction, and you bail them out every time they are in trouble, you are feeding that giant in their life.

The Canaanite is a giant of carnal excess and dissolution. *The Webster's Revised Unabridged Dictionary* defines "dissolution" as "destruction of anything by the separation of its parts; ruin or the corruption of morals; dissipation." *The Strong's Exhaustive Concordance* defines it as "the breaking up of a journey" (2646). In Genesis 13, Abraham and Lot were rich, but their servants were fighting, so they decided to separate. Lot chose to live in the Canaanite city of Sodom, which was more attractive. It was "sin city"—an opportunity to live an alternative lifestyle—away from God.

The Canaanite giant places a high emphasis on beautiful things. They value soulish relationships more than the things of God. Scripture says Lot lived in the cities of the plains toward Sodom. The word "plain" that appears in this passage is translated from the Hebrew word *kikkar*, which comes from the Hebrew word *karar*, oddly enough meaning "to whirl, to dance" (*Strong's Hebrew* 3769).

The Canaanite giant influences us to flirt with our destiny—to dance, but never commit and make decisions—only to leave dreams unfulfilled. Listening to the giant's lies, we sin and say, "I couldn't help myself. I thought it was over. I thought you weren't coming back. You made me do this. I was born like this."

Unmasked

Several years ago, I attended New Life's "Every Man's Battle Workshop" to improve my integrity as a husband, father, and man of God. One of the things I was challenged to do at the meeting was to disclose my life story to my wife, making myself fully known and sharing all the things I had hidden from her—from the attempted sexual assault when I was eight to the promiscuous lifestyle in my teenage years—that had left doors to lust and sin open in my life.

The facilitator challenged the men: "Tell her, because 'your' story has been 'her' story." Give full disclosure with no statute of limitations. They challenged us to take our masks off. We all wear them. As creatures of habit, we all show some parts of ourselves and hide others. We project a persona of what we think other people want to see and wear masks to hide the parts we are ashamed of. Masks are ways we keep ourselves from being fully known to people. They allow us to take on the identity of someone completely different while remaining the same inside.

What are some of the masks you wear?

Here are some examples discussed at the conference:

- **The All Together Mask**: I want you to think I'm ok. I'm afraid that if you know the truth, it will expose that I don't have it all together.
- **The Superman Mask**: I am super. Bulletproof. Invincible. Nothing hurts me. We wear this to avoid shame or pain.
- **The Busy Mask**: I keep myself busy to avoid you seeing the mess I am truly in.
- **The Sports Mask**: I am always coaching a team or someone's kid. Playing in fantasy sports leagues. Refereeing in leagues. Always working on someone else's game except mine. I hide behind this mask in pretense—pretending to be someone else (*e.g.*, Phil Jackson, Bill Belichick, Michael Jordan, Tom Brady).
- **The CEO Mask**: I am running a company. Organizing a team. Evaluating employees. Giving orders. But not taking them. I have no one to speak into my life as I pour into others.
- **The Joker Mask**: I am the comedian—the life of every party. I make jokes about my insecurities.

Weight. Looks. Position. Co-workers. Boss or salary.

- **The Pastor/Ministry Mask**: I am counseling, preaching, praying for people, and building everyone else, while my life or family is falling apart.
- **The Spiderman Mask**: I am in the relentless pursuit of revenge. Always looking to get back at people. This mask never admits the hurt or pain people cause. It pursues vendettas instead of victory.

What would happen if we lived without masks? Rick Warren once said: "Wearing a mask wears you out."

I'll admit, initially at the conference, I was excited about the prospect of being free—to remove my mask(s). Many of the things I never exposed and confronted in life were tearing my marriage apart. But I was nervous and uncomfortable with the challenge, and shame was the culprit. I thought I was over some things in life, but that too was a mask. As long as we keep masks on, we don't have to admit weaknesses. We don't have to show the effect of something, someone, or who we really are. We often try to be strong for everyone. But we don't have to be strong for God. We can come boldly—just as we are. In a mess. With tears, flaws, fears, and questions. God said, "In our weakness, his strength is made perfect" (2 Corinthians 12:9).

At the conference, they also asked us to write down eight to ten things we wish we heard growing up or as an adult. All of mine were from my childhood with my parents. I wanted my wife to fill the deficits not filled by my mom and dad. I was trying to confirm my masculinity in her femininity—walking around with a little boy still crying inside of me—engaging in silent wars. Trying to transfer to my wife everything I feel that hurts, feels inadequate, screams disrespect, insignificance, and failure.

As I prepared to come home and talk to her, God encouraged me to unmask myself through Genesis 2:24-25: "This explains why a man leaves his father and mother and is joined to his wife, and the two are united into one. Now the man and his wife were both naked, *but they felt no shame*" (NLT, emphasis added).

The only way Adam and Eve felt no shame is when they were both naked—fully known and transparent. As long as sin and shame were present, they hid. Too often, we hide our true selves. We create masks or hide behind sewn fig leaves because of some shame we are carrying from our past. Shame is a dream killer. It creates a mask for us to hide behind.

In Genesis 2, Adam and Eve sin and immediately feel shame. They use trees to try and cover themselves—to hide. But God comes walking in the "cool" of the day. Not the "heat" of the day. Not angry. But with a simple question, "Where are you?" The first Adam hid behind a tree. The second Adam—Jesus—hung on a tree.

Today, what mask are you hiding behind? The work you do, the positions you hold, the fame or wealth you acquire, the ministries you serve in, the pain you disclose can all serve as masks. But there is freedom living unveiled, unmasked, and unashamed. As long as secrets exist, there will be shame. Shame keeps us from pursuing the call of God on our life. But Jesus removes shame to restore honor.

Dr. Brene Brown once wrote, "You can choose courage or you can choose comfort. But you cannot have both. In the arena you enter, there are always box seats. There are always the seats in the arena, occupied by the people who built the arena, to benefit those who look and act like the people who built the arena. In life, there will be people already booing and expecting you to fail. Don't assign that feeling to shame."

When we are transparent, we tell the story that people are already living in our lives. We let our lives go, to save it (Luke 17:33 NLT).

The pieces of our life we withhold from God keep us incomplete. But if we give Him everything, God will conclude this chapter and start a new one. He will flip the page and write a new ending in our life. He will finish this book. As the author and finisher of our faith, He is not writing a horror or fiction story. He's writing a heroic, inspirational book of faith. And no matter what chapter of life we are in, He has written more. No matter what our marriage looks like, what our health and career feel like, He has written more. God has more in store for us. He has written a bestseller about us and our story is going to top the charts. It's going to inspire dozens, hundreds, thousands, or millions we can't see right now.

Flirting with Destiny

No matter how talented and gifted we are, there will always be people who want us to fail. Don't assign that giant to shame. Don't dance or flirt with your destiny. March towards it. In the book of Exodus, the Canaanite giant influenced a blessed, marching people to build a golden calf—to dance and have a party while separated from Moses.

Moses was furious:

When they came near the camp, Moses saw the calf and the dancing, and he burned with anger. He threw the stone tablets to the ground, smashing them at the foot of the mountain. He took the calf they had made and burned it. Then he ground it into powder, threw it into the water, and forced the people to drink it. Finally, he turned to Aaron and demanded, "What did these people do to you to make you bring such terrible sin upon them?" "Don't get so upset, my lord," Aaron replied. "You yourself know how evil these people are. They said to me, 'Make us gods who will lead us. We don't know what happened to this fellow Moses, who brought us here from the land of Egypt.' So I told them, 'Whoever has gold jewelry, take it off.' When they brought it to me, I simply threw it into the fire—and out came this calf!" Moses saw that Aaron had let the people get completely out of control, much to the amusement of their enemies. So he stood at the entrance to the camp and shouted, "All of you who are on the Lord's side, come here and join me." And all the Levites gathered around him. (Exodus 32:19-26)

Idolatry is a dream killer. Don't amuse Satan with your sin. Choose what side you are on. My family and the victims who died in Jonestown chose the wrong side. They flirted with the devil. They made Jim Jones their idol. But on the fateful night of the massacre, Jones sent his children away and killed theirs.

The Canaanite giant is unruly and truly unrestrained. It is out of control. It is constantly worried about what people might think—blaming others or parents for their bad decisions. The Canaanite distorts our wishes to please others—through masks—to become something we never intended to be. If you are struggling with the Canaanite giant in your life, you must be willing to commit yourself to its destruction—without compromise—or you will not be able to stand before your enemies. (See Joshua 7:1-15).

In Deuteronomy 29:23, the author wrote this about the fate of those who stay in a wilderness of bad decisions: "The whole land is brimstone and salt, a burning waste, unsown and unproductive, and no grass grows in it; it is like the overthrow of Sodom and Gomorrah, Admah and Zeboiim, which the Lord overthrew in His anger and wrath."

The Israelites wandered in an infertile wilderness for forty years. Nothing grew there, because it was never to be their home. It was a testing ground. One of the indications of temporary residency is barrenness. God has promised us lands of milk and honey—hills and valleys. Anything less than that is temporary. It is only a test. Just as between every new mountaintop there is a valley, between Egypt and Jericho there was a wilderness or desert experience. God demanded total obedience from the Israelites while nothing was growing. When He gave them manna, they asked, "What is it?" But every day, they had to wake up and collect just enough for the day, then go to sleep, wake up, and repeat. They hated the manna (Numbers 11:1-4). They complained about it daily. "It's still the same. Nothing has changed. It's still manna."

Likewise, you may look at your life and feel, "It's still the same job. Same business. Same marriage. Same addiction." But God is building consistency. He makes us something when we are nothing. He builds a name in us that makes giants cringe with fear.

The apostle Paul once asked this question: "What benefit (return) did you get from the things of which you are now ashamed?" (Romans 6:21).

What was the benefit of your worst decision or failure? I don't care what you have done—what has happened in your life—where you have failed. You are not damaged goods. You are not a mistake. You will not die in the wilderness. You will enter into the land of your dreams and promise. Because no past defines us. Our choices do. God does. Don't live a life created by bad decisions, or by what someone did to you. Live by what Jesus did for you.

My pastor once said, "God can take the worst thing that ever happened to you, pour his grace upon it, and make it the best thing that ever happened to you."

Today, God is doing a "new thing" (Isa. 43:18-19).

He does a new thing after the worst thing has happened. He makes a way in the driest and darkest places in your life.

Make. A. Way.

Blaze a trail. Do something new. Spring forth.

I declare, you will forget the shame of your past. You will not be disgraced. You will not suffer humiliation. You will win. You were born into a lineage of giant (and addiction) killers. City takers. Lion mouth stoppers. Red Sea splitters. Pit overcomers. Palace presidents and grave raisers.

The lineage of Jesus Christ was both from God and humanity. He was an earthly descendant of:

- David, a giant killer.
- Rahab, the prostitute who saved the two spies with a scarlet cord.
- Joshua, who tore down the walls of Jericho.
- Zerubbabel, who built a temple.
- Boaz, who was the redeemer kinsman.
- Jacob, who dreamed of heaven touching earth.
- Isaac, who was the child of promise.
- Abraham, who was the father of faith—the friend of God.

God takes what is little or despised in our family tree to make it great in our lifetime.

But he also can take the good part of our family's history and build legacy with it: "Listen to me, all who hope for deliverance—all who seek the Lord! Consider the rock from which you were cut, the quarry from which you were mined. Yes, think about Abraham, your ancestor, and Sarah, who gave birth to your nation. Abraham was only one man when I called him. But when I blessed him, he became a great nation" (Isaiah 51:1-2 NLT).

When tough times come, look to the Rock from which you were hewn. It is a Rock that stands. Water, creativity, and strength flow from this Rock. It will not be moved. We have a heritage of small beginnings becoming a great nation. Of little, inferior men and women defeating giants. Disarmed armies taking walled cities. And because of our history, we can win.

CHAPTER 7

THE GIANT OF LAZINESS

Perizzites: Belonging to a village. Limited vision or dreams. Laziness. Low self-esteem.

Have you ever made a vow hastily or broken one?

Every New Year's, we make resolutions on certain things we've failed to finish, accomplish, or get rid of in our lives. Sadly, we don't always finish what we start. We fail to complete tasks. Stick to diets. Read all the chapters in a book. Stay on exercise routines. Complete recovery steps. Get out of debt. Lose weight. Restore the broken marriage or relationship.

We are consistently inconsistent in some areas, not realizing every new year is the fruit of 365 days sown in the previous year. A harvest of our past decisions— the past year of our lives. A new beginning to assimilate everything we have learned into new strategies, parenting, processes, ideas, relationship building, goals, and dreams.

By now, we know what works and what doesn't. For example, I know what will drop pounds and what will add pounds to my frame—regardless of my discipline or lack thereof to do it. I know how to make peace or start war with my wife. What tasks are productive at work and what are time wasters. How to be powerful or passive in ministry. We know what needs to change in our lives, whether we change it or not. And that daily routine in our lives is either killing or strengthening our dreams and relationships.

Have you clearly heard God about changing an area of your life, but have not followed through? Are you cohabitating with the giant of laziness? Struggling to keep the commitments you make? Discouraged from even trying?

Currently, I am the president of ERN Enterprises, Inc. and The National Council of Reimbursement Advocacy. We advocate for medically appropriate healthcare for patients and providers pursuant to a case called *Wickline vs. State*. We fight HMOs and third-party payers that make negligent utilization decisions to improperly deny care and claims to providers. Our team of advocates have helped hundreds of thousands of patients. We have done pro bono cases to help save or improve patient lives, including but not limited to:

- A stage four breast cancer patient given only weeks to live
- A young boy with one leg eleven inches shorter than the other gets a leg-lengthening surgery
- A young infant with a disease that mimics polio gets the care initially denied as experimental, and so many more

I often encourage our team, "We may not have a 100% success rate, but we fight each case as if we had never lost. Don't ever be discouraged in doing the right thing. Do the things you can control. You can't control giants or problem HMOs. But you can control how you fight them. Sow seeds when you feel unfruitful. Keep showing up as if you never failed. Keep putting appeals in the pipeline. Knocking on doors. Finding supporting documents and arguments to fight. Finding hospitals to entrust us with more human lives. The hearts of some payers are hardened, but they can be turned. Keep striking the ground."

Strike the Ground

What does that mean?

This concept is found in 2 Kings:

When Elisha was in his last illness, King Jehoash of Israel visited him and wept over him. "My father! My father! I see the chariots and charioteers of Israel!" he cried. Elisha told him, "Get a bow and some arrows." And the king did as he was told. Elisha told him, "Put your hand on the bow," and Elisha laid his own hands on the king's hands. Then he commanded, "Open that eastern window," and he opened it. Then he said, "Shoot!" So he shot an arrow. Elisha proclaimed, "This is the Lord's arrow, an arrow of victory over Aram, for you will completely conquer the Arameans at Aphek." Then he said, "Now pick up the other arrows and strike them against the ground." So the king picked them up and struck the ground three times. But the man of God was angry with him. "You should have struck the ground five or six times!" he exclaimed. "Then you would have beaten Aram until it was entirely destroyed. Now you will be victorious only three times. (2 Kings 13:14-19 NLT)

How many times do we strike the ground and stop?

We only apply to three schools. Apply for three jobs. Stop smoking or drinking for three days. Take the state bar or certification exam three times. Ask for a promotion or raise three years—then stop. We feel it is useless to keep trying, so we only strike three times—then stop. We don't hit the ground repeatedly with our best. We are inconsistent and fall short in achieving what God predestined for our life.

We may even go through the motions to give a modest appearance of trying before we quit, just so we can say, "We tried." Too often, we want a quick, guaranteed victory before we commit to giving our best. We wait for people to offer us a promotion before we do our best to earn one. We expect people to promote us as a leader, before we become one. We expect people to find us, instead of seizing opportunities.

What have you stopped doing your best in?

Whatever is lackluster, lazy, or inconsistent in your life is the Perizzite giant. The Perizzite giants were "villagers" or "dwellers" who lived in the land of promise. Perizzite means, "belonging to a village." A village is distinguished from a town by the lack of a market (*KJB Dictionary*). People who grow up in villages have different resources for growth, education, culture, and entertainment. Opportunity may be scarce. Perizzites often limit themselves in life, have low self-esteem, or lack confidence, making them less likely to dream great things. They see themselves as people with little potential—whose task in life is to stay out of the way of people who are "really" important.

Civil Rights Activist Oscar Wright, a regular speaker at the Jonestown Memorial Services, once said, "We have trained instead of educated our children. Education is a combination of high academic skills with high social and spiritual values propelled by common sense—utilizing God-given wisdom to think and reason. Exposure is education. Trained people do what you tell them to do, sometimes lacking common sense to be critical thinkers. But educated people think for themselves."

The Israelites suffered from this in Egypt—limited vision. Lack of exposure. Trained in hard labor, they lived in deplorable conditions. But after 400 years of slavery, God was still watching over them to fulfill His promise. He remembered the promise He made to them and responded to their cry with a family—two men and one woman—Moses, Aaron, and Miriam to demand the release of their dreams held hostage (Micah 6:4).

In Exodus 5, we see the initial reaction from Pharaoh—the Israelite's giant—and Israel's response:

> "Moses and Aaron, why are you distracting the people from their tasks? Get back to work! Look, there are many of your people in the land, and you are stopping them from their work." That same day Pharaoh sent this order to the Egyptian slave drivers and the Israelite foremen: "Do not supply any more straw for making bricks. Make the people get it themselves! But still require them to make the same number of bricks as before. Don't reduce the quota. They are lazy. That's why they are crying out, 'Let us go and offer sacrifices to our God.' Load them down with more work. Make them sweat! That will teach them to listen to lies!" …The Israelite foremen could see that they were in serious trouble when they were told, "You must not reduce the number of bricks you make each day." As they left Pharaoh's court, they confronted Moses and Aaron, who were waiting outside for them. The foremen said to them, "May the Lord judge and punish you for making us stink before Pharaoh and his officials. You have put a sword into their hands, an excuse to kill us!" (Exodus 5: 4-9,19-21 NLT)

Limited vision will keep you stagnant, staying in one place. Egypt trained the Israelites how to live. They were hostages, not educated in God's best for their lives. When Moses confronted Pharaoh, things got worse before they got better. Their taskmasters called them lazy and beat them for not producing their daily numbers. They took their straw away and mocked them: "Why haven't you met your quota of bricks yesterday or today, as before?" (v.14).

But God refused to allow the Israelites to remain in Egypt. Moses said to Pharaoh, "If we don't leave Egypt— if we stay where we are, God will strike us down with plagues" (v. 3). God sees. He hears. He loves us too much to leave us in a place we feel unappreciated. But lazy, limited faith won't birth the dreams in our heart.

I hired an attorney some years ago, who used to play volleyball for Loyola Marymount, a Division I college in California. He wasn't a starter. But his coach told him to remember two things before he went into each game:

1. Know the score of the game.
   and
2. When you come out of the game, the score must have changed.

I love that. He didn't just tell his players to have fun or do their best. He challenged them to be a difference-maker—a game-changer.

How do we change the score of the game? How can we make our family, team, church, or organization better? What are we doing daily towards our dream? Have we set goals or quotas to build the vision in our hearts?

By now, we know success is not an overnight thing. What comes in our lives—a new contract, new job, new strategy, dreams and promises fulfilled, good things—will not be instantaneous. It will be a culmination of every-thing sowed, dreamed, hoped, prayed for, imagined, cried over, grieved about, tried, and failed over the past year or decade. Everything we sacrificed for.

Created to Thrive

King Solomon wrote in Proverbs 13:19," Souls who follow their hearts thrive" (MSG). You cannot thrive unless you do what God has put in your heart.

You may have a career or be in school studying a major, but if it is a loveless affair and not a love connec-tion, you cannot maximize your potential for success. My late great-grandmother Julie used to love the show *Love Connection*. The show would pair a single contestant with three contestants of the opposite sex behind a curtain, and then ask questions to try and match them.

We need to ask questions. We must go on fact-finding missions to determine what we love, and how to get people to pay us to do it. That means, we don't choose a degree that does not follow our heart. We don't work the rest of our life in something we hate or something that doesn't repre-sent what we are called to do—allowing us to do our best work. Get involved in an area of the church. Volunteer at a non-profit. Do something that represents your heart. The people in Nehemiah built the wall in an area close to home—close to their own heart (Nehemiah 3:1-32).

God wants our soul to thrive. And He has given us a "thrive book." The Bible helps us to thrive spiritually, physically, and emotionally. Thrive in our families. Thrive in business and school. Thrive in the house of God. Thrive mentally, because "So as a man thinks, so is he" (Pro. 23:7). That word "thrive" means to "flourish, prosper, increase, be blessed or favored; to have a flourishing life." My brother-in-law, Gabriel and his company Marquet, once did an intensive at our church and asked a staffer, "Are you excellent in what you do?" The staffer replied, "I'm anointed so I don't need to be excellent."

But Daniel thrived in captivity. Taken by unlawful force and criticized by his peers, Daniel and his four friends were ten times better than those educated in the language and literature of the Babylonians (Daniel 1:20).

In Jeremiah 29:5-7, God exhorts His children to thrive in exile:

> Build houses and settle down; plant gardens and eat what they produce. Marry and have sons and daughters; find wives for your sons and give your daughters in marriage, so that they too may have sons and daughters. Increase in number there; do not decrease. Also, seek the peace and prosperity of the city to which I have carried you into exile. Pray to the Lord for it, because if it prospers, you too will prosper.

God expects us to thrive in our created purpose—to be fruitful and multiply—no matter where we are. If we get depressed or despondent quickly because of opposition, we will not thrive. We will waste away without a fight, without strength to defy our environment.

Today, God wants us to build in a place that is not our own, so that He can make something grow in a strange place. A strange season. A strange job or time in our life that doesn't make sense.

You can thrive now.

Grow Like a Cedar

Living a flourishing life is a thriving life. God has called you to grow like a cedar, not a twig—even in old age (Psalm 92:12-14).

Abraham waited long and endured patiently. But Isaac, the son of his old age—the son of the supernatural—was still not the full promise. He was a down payment—a multiplier in Abraham's old age of what was to come. Obedience adds to your life; disobedience subtracts. God added Isaac, to subtract Ishmael, then He multiplied Abraham through Isaac.

Whatever God asks us to do is designed to multiply. Multiply the productivity of our workplace. The clients of our business. Souls saved. People reached or discipled in our churches. The dreams and faith of our children. God called us, wherever we are, *to multiply*.

In Exodus, we see a new king, who knew nothing of Joseph, come to power in Egypt. Seeing the Israelites were too numerous and more powerful than the Egyptians, he appointed Egyptian taskmasters to oppress and work the Israelites ruthlessly. He made their lives bitter with hard labor in brick and mortar. Every task he imposed was harsh. He was a giant.

Exodus 1:12-13 says, "But the more the Egyptians oppressed them, the more the Israelites multiplied and spread, and the more alarmed the Egyptians became. So, the Egyptians worked the people of Israel without mercy. They made their lives bitter, forcing them to mix mortar and make bricks and do all the work in the fields. They were ruthless in all their demands" (NLT).

You can thrive in ruthless environments.

Thriving is to grow stronger with an unshakable commitment to a place (*e.g.*, your job, school, a church)—no matter who is in charge. Therefore, whatever you intend to thrive in, must be intentional. You cannot succeed and be lazy at the same time.

I love the story of Joseph, the dreamer. Even though he was sold into slavery, bitterly betrayed, stripped of his coat of many colors, thrown into a well, then sold out by his own family, God was setting the stage for Joseph to rule in Egypt. In a foreign place, God kept him safe and groomed him for his destiny.

Genesis 39:5-6 says, "From the time he put him in charge of his household and of all that he owned, the Lord blessed the household of the Egyptian because of Joseph. The blessing of the Lord was on everything Potiphar had, both in the house and in the field. So, Potiphar left everything he had in Joseph's care; with Joseph in charge, he did not concern himself with anything except the food he ate" (NIV).

Can you be entrusted to work in excellence, without supervision, over things put into your care? Right now, are you thriving and growing in your life? As a husband? A wife? A parent? A son or daughter? A sibling? An employee? A student? An athlete? A business owner or pastor? God did not promote Joseph until he was able to prove growth and consistency over a course of time.

A few things about growth:

- Growth does not happen automatically.
- Growth does not happen quickly.
- Growth does not happen mysteriously—it is intentional.

Recently, I met a former business owner who owned a photography company, taking school photos in all of Los Angeles County. While asking advice about investment properties, he shared that for decades he built a business enabling him to corner the market share of his region. No one could get in and steal schools or clients from him. After forty years, he sold the business and signed a no-compete agreement in exchange for half-a-million dollars every four months (for a length of time). God reminded me I had only been in business for twenty years. I still had twenty years to grow and get to where he was.

We thrive in the waiting periods of our lives. You don't grow without soil, water, care, and tending. You must tend the ground you have.

Here are seven habits of people who grow:

1. They eat the Word of God.
2. They breathe strong with prayer.
3. They purify the soul.
4. They love like Jesus.
5. They forgive daily.
6. They build relationships.
7. They learn to give.

Have you grown to become all you thought you would be by now?

Can you make bricks (results) without bosses giving you straw (resources)?

Someone once said: "Love not what you are but what you may become."

What is your quota to:

- write chapters daily?
- exercise daily?
- read daily?
- make basketball shots daily?

In our story, the Israelites stopped meeting their quotas. They were discouraged. The work was harder. Pharaoh's heart was cold and hardened towards them. It seemed unfair. They were hostile standards to work in, but God was in it. They were His chosen people. Anointed, set apart, called to thrive. Setback to be set up for a great exodus from the worst place in their lives to what God promised. God was using this harsh place to show His outstretched arm and power to save them—to prepare them for a great deliverance.

But they couldn't see it, no matter how much He tried to tell them: "So Moses told the people of Israel what the Lord had said, but they refused to listen anymore. They had become too discouraged by the brutality of their slavery" (Exodus 6:9 NLT).

Sometimes we can't see what God is doing. We get discouraged because of a hostile environment we are in. It seems things will never change, so we stop producing daily or lower our standards. We become distracted. Unfocused. But just because people won't change doesn't mean you should change your work ethic. Just because people won't acknowledge or promote you doesn't mean you should stop trying to be qualified for the job. Just because that coach doesn't recognize your efforts doesn't mean you should stop trying to exceed them. Just because a professor grades you unfairly doesn't mean you shouldn't be better and produce your best work. Just because you are oppressed, doesn't mean you can't multiply. You were created to do awesome work, so people can stand in awe of you. To do something you have never done before—to be something you have never been before—despite the giants in your life.

The Perizzite giant deceives us into believing because time has passed, what God promised has expired. But it has not expired. No matter how many years you have waited, no matter how much you have failed or lost faith, God is still big enough to bring down the biggest giant in your life.

The author of Hebrews encourages us with this:

So God's rest is there for people to enter, but those who first heard this good news failed to enter because they disobeyed God. So, God set another time for entering his rest, and that time is today. God announced this through David much later in the words already quoted: "Today when you hear his voice, don't harden your hearts." Now if Joshua had succeeded in giving them this rest, God would not have spoken about another day of rest still to come. So, there is a special rest still waiting for the people of God. For all who have entered into God's rest have rested from their labors, just as God did after creating the world. So let us do our best to enter that rest. But if we disobey God, as the people of Israel did, we will fall. (Hebrews 4:6-11 NLT)

Your. Time. Is. Today.

Even when you have failed, been faithless, not thrived or when you are not following your heart due to circumstances or raising children, God keeps renewing the promise and setting the date as today. In our old age, there is still an opportunity to enter what He promised. Our kids can possess the things we failed to. And if they fail, God can start the clock all over again.

My writing mentor's great-grandfather helped found an evangelistic branch of the Mennonite Church in Ukraine, whose aggressive evangelizing resulted over time in one-third of Mennonites in Ukraine becoming committed Christians. Today, there are five generations among the Stobbe descendants who almost all are still active Christians.

Moses's task was difficult because no one believed God could do what He promised, what they lost hope waiting for. There will be times in life where it seems our disobedience, mistakes, and fears have caused us to miss our window of opportunity. The devil tells us, "It's too late. You will always be like this." But we still have a "live" promise. God kept the Israelites alive in the calamity of slavery and subsequently in the wilderness for a reason. He wasn't finished with them yet. He's not finished with us either. He has kept us alive despite bad relationships. Business losses. Sicknesses or a bad prognosis. And the Israelite story is proof God can take something medi-ocre, impoverished, and enslaved in bondage to make it glorious. Make it great. Make it thrive. Make it a strong army of giant killers.

Paralyzed As a Child

Have you ever felt something was owed to you or taken unlawfully?

Mephibosheth, Saul's grandson, wanted to be king but was paralyzed by traumatic events from his past. 2 Samuel 9:1-4 records:

> One day David asked, "Is anyone in Saul's family still alive—anyone to whom I can show kindness for Jonathan's sake?" He summoned a man named Ziba, who had been one of Saul's servants. "Are you Ziba?" the king asked. "Yes sir, I am," Ziba replied. The king then asked him, "Is anyone still alive from Saul's family? If so, I want to show God's kindness to them." Ziba replied, "Yes, one of Jonathan's sons is still alive. He is crippled in both feet." "Where is he?" the king asked. "In Lo-debar," Ziba told him, "at the home of Makir son of Ammiel. (NLT)

"Lo-debar" was a dismal place of no pasture, no hope, no word—suggesting a lack of vision (See Hosea 1:6-9). During the reign of King David, Mephibosheth, the son of David's best friend Jonathan and grandson of King Saul, was five years old when his father and grandfather died in battle. The child's nurse, fleeing the war in haste from the royal residence, fell and dropped the child on the ground, paralyzing him from the waist down.

He later found refuge in Lo-Debar. But despite his royal lineage, Mephibosheth felt like a "no-body" in comparison to others. Crippled by life's circumstances, he was unable to dream, get up, and walk on his own. But even if that's you today, your limited vision does not keep God from finding you. No matter how lame your life is, no matter who dropped you, God is looking for a reason to bless you, a source or way to repay you for the covenant you kept. Because when you had every reason to quit and give up, you didn't. When you lost everything, you still trusted and loved Him. You still went to church. You got up every morning for work. You exceeded your quotas—what others asked of you. You stayed committed to the marriage. You raised your children. You served. You loved and forgave. You were faithful. You kept your mouth shut. You didn't complain. And right now, God has initiated a search party to bless you—to overtake you with the unfailing, unsought, unlimited mercy, and kindness of God.

King David found Mephibosheth and gave him all the property that once belonged to his grandfather Saul. He invited him to eat regularly at the king's table (v.7). But when David's family was falling apart, during Absalom's rebellion, Mephibosheth showed his heart. His giant surfaced. He declared, "Today I will get back the kingdom of my grandfather Saul" (2 Samuel 16:3 NLT).

Mephibosheth had more than he ever had before— yet still wanted more. He wanted the kingdom he felt was rightfully his. He didn't know about the covenant his father Jonathan made with David in 1 Samuel 18:3, but he was Saul's grandson. Although lame, in his heart, he still wanted to be king. The regrets of being dropped from the lineage—not being on the throne at five—was still affecting him years later in his adult life. There was royalty in his blood, but also bad family history. Our giants, the handicaps we live with, will either empower or entitle us in life.

My youngest son Josiah is a college football athlete at UCLA. As a junior in high school, he transferred from Troy High School (Division V) to Santa Margarita Catholic High School in the Trinity League (Division I), arguably the toughest league in the nation. He had his best season statistically as a senior that year. But as a smaller quarterback (5'10), Josiah had only four Division I college offers. Recruiters ignored his resume, labeling his size a handicap. As an All-Trinity QB with league awards, he put up the most points of any opponent, all season, against the 2018 Mater Dei championship team—arguably the best high school football team assembled in the California Interscholastic Federation's (CIF) history—but coaches "slept on him" because of his size. I kept telling him to go to West Point (one of his offers)—where his recruitment was the strongest. But Josiah was empowered to prove himself in California. He repeatedly told me, "I will get another offer to play on the West Coast." While trying to help him understand the reality of what was happening, I was careful not to discourage him, as I have heard that males in their adolescence experience a hormone released in the brain that makes them fearless and courageous.

Josiah is one of the hardest working people I know. We never had to tell him to work out, practice, or do the extra things to get better. He is relentless and wants to be the best at whatever he put his hands to. (In the fifth grade, without ever riding a horse, he won a rodeo competition at a school camp). We would have supported his dream no matter what school he chose.

In January of Josiah's senior year, with only four Division I college offers on the table, UCLA called him and offered him a preferred walk-on spot at quarterback. He spoke with coach Chip Kelly and took the offer, bypassing the other four, so in his words he "could become better quicker, stay close to home, and attend one of his dream schools." He chose to thrive in a hostile "preferred walk on" environment, instead of a friendly "recruited" one. We are so proud of his fearlessness—who he is becoming in Christ.

Courage is a necessity in life. Richard Avarmenko, who teaches political science at the University of Wisconsin once wrote, "Courage... is the willingness to risk life and limb for the sake of something." In other words, courage reveals what we care about and reveals what we are willing to lay our life down for.

Jesus Performs Late Miracles

Everything in life will not be on our timetable. Jesus performs "late" miracles all the time. Miracles in finances. Miracles in college or job offers. Miracles in healing that are time sensitive—even when the diagnosis is terminal.

Many people waited until the last hour before Jesus healed them. The woman bound in infirmity in Luke 13:16 was crippled eighteen years. The woman with the issue of blood in Luke 8:43-48 had suffered many things of many physicians and was no better, but rather grew worse. She was sick for twelve years with a hemorrhage. The man at the pool of Bethesda was sick thirty-eight years, but had no man to put him in the water when it rippled. All waited—hoping for a miracle.

How long have you been waiting? Waiting for your healing? Waiting for your spouse or marriage to change? Waiting for the right person to come along? Waiting for the business funding or vision to take off? Waiting for the promotion, raise, or financial breakthrough?

Sometimes we give up after one week. One month. One year. We strike the ground only three times. We don't repeatedly work with our best because we are discouraged. But what is impossible with man, is possible with God (Luke 18:27).

If a person is sick and seeks no medical attention, in the final stages of the disease's progression, feelings of bitter regret can begin. But it is the glory of God to heal those who come late to Him. Jesus can heal what is terminal and irretrievably broken in our lives, no matter how late or what stage we are in life. He can stop us from taking our own lives. He can use us to save someone ready to give up—to raise something dead back to life.

Jesus heals "late." It's in His DNA. He gives us the creativity to save the business about to fail. Solve a company or industry problem. Discover cures. Have hope against hope when the prognosis is poor, and all hope is gone. When the marriage is on the verge of divorce. When your spouse's heart—or yours—has grown cold. When the relationship is strained. When your money isn't enough to cover the bills, even though you have faithfully tithed. Jesus heals late.

Though life is not perfect, God invades our life with perfect timing. He is a flawless and perfect shelter in times of trouble. A perfect love that drives out all fear. In the imperfection of our lives, He is perfect in all of his ways.

Several years ago, my uncle-in-law died from cancer. As I talked to his son the night before the funeral, he told me, "Eddie, I never lost hope for my dad. When his blood pressure dropped, when they took the oxygen mask off, I never lost hope that God could still heal him."

Hope never shames us. Hope strengthens us. King David declared, "What [what would have become of me] had I not believed that I would see the Lord's goodness in the land of the living! Wait and hope for and expect the Lord; be brave and of good courage and let your heart be stout and enduring. Yes, wait for and hope for and expect the Lord" (Psalm 27:13-14 AMPC).

The apostle Paul wrote:

- "Even when there was no reason for hope, Abraham kept hoping—believing that he would become the father of many nations. For God had said to him, 'That's how many descendants you will have!' And

Abraham's faith did not weaken, even though, at about 100 years of age, he figured his body was as good as dead—and so was Sarah's womb" (Romans 4:18-19 NLT).

- "Such hope never disappoints or deludes or shames us, for God's love has been poured out in our hearts through the Holy Spirit Who has been given to us" (Romans 5:5 AMP).
- "Christ in you, [is] the hope of glory" (Colossians 1:27 NIV).

It is the glory of God to raise, save, and heal us no matter what happens to this earthly body. Keep your weapons drawn. Keep praying for the miracle. Keep trusting God's promise—no matter how old you are. How late it is. Don't stop until you get it.

We can't shortchange ourselves. As giant killers, we must take risks. Striking that giant of lazy faith until our bad habits are crushed and defeated. Asking God to put His hands on ours. To give us a rematch—a stunning victory in the areas we are defeated. Don't treat opposition as a reason to quit. We can't use trouble as a sign to stop doing what God has called us to—to stop praying. We can't let failure—after one loss—question our calling (See Exodus 5:22-23).

As Elisha told King Jehoash in 2 Kings 13:14-19, keep striking the ground. God wants faith—trust that strikes the ground repeatedly before the results are seen. The striking is the process before the dream or promise is

fulfilled. This is not a time to be indecisive, to be inconsistent—to complain and murmur. Keep gathering straw.
Keep making bricks. Keep meeting daily quotas. Keep
thriving. Despite the hostile demands on our lives, a great
exodus is coming.

CHAPTER 8

THE GIANT OF PROCRASTINATION

Hivites: Villagers. Vision is limited to enjoying an earthly inheritance. The pursuit of pleasure. Sensual self-indulgence.

Mark Twain once said, "If the first thing you do each morning is to eat a live frog, you can go through the day with the satisfaction of knowing that is probably the worst thing that is going to happen to you all day long."

Our "frog" is the worst thing imaginable we must do. It is the thing we are most afraid of. The most unpleasant task. The passivity that breeds temptation. The step of faith we don't take. The business idea or invention we don't pursue. The ministry we never start. The improved spouse or parent we never become. The marriage commitment we never make. The giant (or habit) we are unwilling to confront. It is the most critical thing we habitually put off that impedes our highest dreams.

Havilah Cunnington wrote, "Don't be surprised if the very thing you're scared to do is the very thing you're called to do."

We are not doing all God has called us to do.

The waiting seasons of our lives are worsened by procrastination. Fear and safety prevent us from being who we really are. From fulfilling our destiny. It keeps testing the gap of what we are doing, from what we want, which leads us to the next giant the Israelites had to confront: The Hivite.

When the Israelites escaped Egypt, the Hivites were already firmly established as one of the seven Canaanite nations whose destruction was ordered (Deuteronomy 1:7). But when Joshua and the Israelite army attacked, the men of the Hivite city, Gibeon, tricked Israel into saving them by stating they were not neighbors but had come from a distant country to become their servants.

We read the story in chapter nine of the Book of Joshua:

Now all the kings west of the Jordan River heard about what had happened. These were the kings of the Hittites, Amorites, Canaanites, Perizzites, Hivites, and Jebusites, who lived in the hill country, in the western foothills, and along the coast of the Mediterranean Sea as far north as the Lebanon mountains. These kings combined their armies to fight as one against Joshua and the Israelites. But when the people of Gibeon heard what Joshua had done to Jericho and Ai, *they resorted to deception to save themselves.* They sent ambassadors to Joshua, loading their donkeys with weathered saddlebags and old, patched wineskins. They put

THE GIANT OF PROCRASTINATION

on worn-out, patched sandals and ragged clothes. And the bread they took with them was dry and moldy. When they arrived at the camp of Israel at Gilgal, they told Joshua and the men of Israel, "We have come from a distant land to ask you to make a peace treaty with us." ...So the Israelites examined their food, but they did not consult the Lord. Then Joshua made a peace treaty with them and guaranteed their safety, and the leaders of the community ratified their agreement with a binding oath. Three days after making the treaty, they learned that these people actually lived nearby... Joshua called together the Gibeonites and said, "Why did you lie to us? Why did you say that you live in a distant land when you live right here among us? May you be cursed! From now on you will always be servants who cut wood and carry water for the house of my God." They replied, "We did it because we—your servants—were clearly told that the Lord your God commanded his servant Moses to give you this entire land and to destroy all the people living in it. So we feared greatly for our lives because of you. That is why we have done this. Now we are at your mercy—do to us whatever you think is right." (Joshua 9:1-6, 14-16, 22-25) NLT)

The Hivites pretended to be someone else. They wore old, worn clothing to deceive Joshua into believing that they had been walking or working for a long time. Similar to the Perizzite, the Hivite had a limited outlook on life. They lived deceptively to keep their position of safety at any cost.

Likewise, sometimes we expect old wineskins, or old habits, to open new doors. We seek guarantees without production. Power without performance. Righteousness without right decisions. We say we are something we are not, to be accepted—to arrive, having done nothing to get there. We wear masks to obtain things we didn't work for. We make covenants with habitual sins. But God can't pour what is new on top of what is old. He pours new wine into new wineskins. New perspectives, attitudes, and behaviors. Everything has to be new.

For example, we can't just chase bad thoughts away; we must replace them with new ones. We can't just wish old habits away; we must replace them with new habits. If we procrastinate, we can't just say, "I am not going to be a procrastinator anymore." We have to fill idle space with intentionality. We have to replace habitually putting off things that should be done, by daily "eating our frog."

The Hivite giant steals identity to stay in comfort and to get what they want under false pretenses (e.g., a car loan, credit card, job, client). This person moves from place to place, from job to job, without taking risks or improving themselves. The Hivite wants the freedom to live however they please, and before they lose that right, they will lie to keep it. Procrastination deceives people to save ourselves.

To convince people that we are ok. That we are working on things when we are not.

Don't make a treaty with this giant.

Strength to Possess

In Joshua 3:8-10, Joshua said to the Israelites, "Come here and listen to the words of the Lord your God. This is how you will know that the living God is among you and that he will certainly drive out before you the Canaanites, Hittites, Hivites, Perizzites, Girgashites, Amorites and Jebusites" (NIV).

To be a giant killer, we need two things:

1. Strength to go in
   <u>and</u>
2 Faith inspired by love

Moses told the Israelites: "Therefore, be careful to obey every command I am giving you today, so you may have strength to go in and take over the land you are about to enter" (Deuteronomy 11:8 NLT).

Strength is needed when we don't have any. When we can't see what God is doing. When we are tested. The author in Psalm 105 wrote, "Then he sent someone to Egypt ahead of them—Joseph, who was sold as a slave. They bruised his feet with fetters and placed his neck in an iron collar. Until the time came to fulfill his dreams, the Lord tested Joseph's character" (vv. 17-19 NLT).

We will be tested.

In Exodus 16:15, God allowed the Israelites to be hungry to test them with something they had never seen before (manna)—to see if He could trust them with what He promised.

Can God trust you with favor? With your spouse's or child's heart? With the second chance, city, business or job He gave you? We need strength to possess and to make our eyes, mouths, thoughts, and decisions obey. Because disobedience will keep us in a place where we constantly need someone to feed us.

But sometimes, God will allow a season of confusion—where things don't make sense—to prove and refine our character in weak areas and to help us exercise the weapon of obedience. My wife once told me: "Until our character catches up with our calling, God can't do *all* He has promised us."

The Hivite (giant of procrastination) will keep you wandering in the wilderness when you are tested. Accepting things that we think will never change (*e.g.*, sickness, depression, pain, addiction, anger). Refusing to confront them. Blaming people for where we are in life— whether they are dead or alive. Staying in positions where others put us, but where our heart was not planted, where people dictated who and what we will be. Because when we are passive and disobedient to what is inside of us, we easily fall to temptation.

The children of Israel stayed in the wilderness of welfare until they crossed the Jordan river and engaged in warfare. My wife and I spent early years in our marriage on food stamps, constantly needing handouts or searching for change in couches to redeem at the local supermarket Coinstar machine. I hated it. But in that season, I learned it is not someone else's job to make sure I eat—physically or spiritually. It is not the sole responsibility of my pastor to feed me. The responsibility for spiritual nourishment to kill giants rests in my relationship with God, through Jesus Christ. It is my job, personally, to develop intimacy with Jesus. The strength we need to take over industries, cities, and giants comes from personal obedience in our life. Personal obedience flows from personal responsibility.

Take Your Choice Back

In 2011 when our marriage was on the brink of divorce, my wife Anu and I went to the National Institute of Marriage (NIM), in Branson, Missouri. Our therapist Dr. Kenny Bryant taught me some powerful things in those few life-changing days. Here are a few:

- "We do what we do to get what we want, or to go far away from what we fear. All behavior is goal-driven."
- "You don't have to react to people's reactions or your fears. You have a yard and your wife has a yard. Be responsible for your own garden. Be responsible for the rewiring of your own heart. Put your mask on first. Work on yourself more than each other."

- "Take personal responsibility. No one can make you think, feel, believe and behave. It's your choice. Take your choice back. Be responsible for your actions. Take your eyes off what someone else has done to you. Stop blaming others for how you feel. You are responsible for your thoughts, feelings, beliefs, and behaviors—not your mate's."

At NIM, I learned the power of possessing our highest dreams is taking responsibility for what is incomplete in our lives—not merely hoping things will get better, but taking responsibility for our part in broken or dysfunctional relationships.

Kenny said, "You can be the best Messiah—the best Jesus in the world—and men still crucify you. You can be the best parent, and your children still disobey you. God was the perfect Father, and Adam and Eve—His children—still disobeyed Him."

How much more will we and the next generation fail?

Sometimes we are waiting for our giants to die from old age. But we must kill them. We must kill indecisiveness. If we are not careful, even our "waiting" can be a form of sin and procrastination. Behind every Hivite giant is the land of your greatest dreams. But you have to want to win. You have to want to go in and possess. The Hivites wore old clothing and sandals to deceive Joshua. Yet the Israelites were on welfare for forty years, and their clothes and shoes did not wear out. God fed them with manna every morning. But the season of welfare didn't end until they stopped procrastinating in the wilderness and crossed the Jordan River.

Procrastination Is Fatal

In Deuteronomy the Lord told His children:

Be careful to obey all the commands I am giving you today. Then you will live and multiply, and you will enter and occupy the land the Lord swore to give your ancestors. Remember how the Lord your God led you through the wilderness for these forty years, humbling you and testing you to prove your character, and to find out whether or not you would obey his commands. Yes, he humbled you by letting you go hungry and then feeding you with manna, a food previously unknown to you and your ancestors. He did it to teach you that people do not live by bread alone; rather, we live by every word that comes from the mouth of the Lord. For all these forty years your clothes didn't wear out, and your feet didn't blister or swell. Think about it: Just as a parent disciplines a child, the Lord your God disciplines you for your own good. "So obey the commands of the Lord your God by walking in his ways and fearing him. For the Lord your God is bringing you into a good land of flowing streams and pools of water, with fountains and springs that gush out in the valleys and hills. It is a land of wheat and barley; of grapevines, fig trees, and pomegranates; of olive oil and honey. It is a land where food is plentiful, and nothing is lacking. (Deuteronomy 8:1-9 NLT)

Where you are going is nothing like where we came from. It is nothing like the life we are living. It resembles nothing of our present or past. Nothing in Egypt. Nothing in the wilderness. It is not the same. It is a place where there is plenty of rain. It is ground that cannot fail—that God waters and tends—that He looks over. It is a place where we're not just dependent on our seed to sow, but God matches our contribution thirty, sixty, and one hundred-fold as a reward for labor in hard places. It is a place that God blesses and keeps his eye on us all year long. A land promised to our obedience. Our changed lifestyle. Pain. Faithfulness. Trust and hope—when there was nothing in the natural to hope for anymore.

Where is your wilderness today?

Who is your giant?

The same sinful, passive decision that cost Adam and Eve their tenancy in the Garden can cost us everything we dream and hope for in life. Goals don't just happen. Decisions we made yesterday, created the life we have today. We can walk in obedience—the blessing God promised—or crawl in sin and procrastination. Albert Einstein once said: "The significant problems we face today cannot be solved at the same level of thinking we were at when we created them."

Faith Works by Love

To be a giant slayer, we need strength to go in. The second thing we need is faith inspired by love.

In Deuteronomy, God continues to exhort His people:

> Be careful to obey all these commands I am giving you. Show love to the Lord your God by walking in his ways and holding tightly to him. Then the Lord will drive out all the nations ahead of you, though they are much greater and stronger than you, and you will take over their land. Wherever you set foot, that land will be yours. Your frontiers will stretch from the wilderness in the south to Lebanon in the north, and from the Euphrates River in the east to the Mediterranean Sea in the west. No one will be able to stand against you, for the Lord your God will cause the people to fear and dread you, as he promised, wherever you go in the whole land. (Deuteronomy 11:22-25 NLT)

God doesn't give us what we dream, wish, or hope for in life just because we want it. Faith requires footsteps. Sometimes, it's scary to take human steps. We show love to God by obeying his Word. By taking supernatural steps when they are not humanly possible. What are some things God has commanded you to walk on? Be careful to march on what He promised. Our blessing flows from obedience, not perfect circumstances (Deuteronomy 28:1-8).

When we are obedient, God releases supernatural strength for us to stand in places where we have fallen, are weak, or powerless. To take over and possess all He has promised. But God doesn't wait for perfect circumstances to do what He promised you. Sometimes He will give you territory for His name's sake. The apostle Paul wrote "You see, at just the right time, when we were still powerless, Christ died for the ungodly" (Romans 5:6 NIV).

All You Can Eat

Moses told the Israelites in Deuteronomy 11:13-15, "If you carefully obey the commands, I am giving you today, and if you love the Lord your God and serve him with all your heart and soul, then he will send the rains in their proper seasons—the early and late rains—so you can bring in your harvests of grain, new wine, and olive oil. He will give you lush pastureland for your livestock, and you yourselves will have all you want to eat" (NLT).

God's promise for us is abundance. Not just enough. Not barely making it. But plenty. Like the Israelites, we have a new home awaiting on the other side of our greatest fears. God sees the hunger and shame we've endured. The time wasted. But He has invested too much into our deliverance to leave us where we are. He won't let us die without a fight—no matter how stubborn we are. As we kill procrastination and leave the place we are, we will have all the food we want on the other side.

When we take over what God has already given us and when we begin to eat the fruit of our own hands, the season of welfare in our life ends and a new season of wealth and possession begins (Joshua 5:2). Our craving to survive will transform into a shout that demands walls come down. Giants will fall. Hearts will melt with fear. And like Caleb at age 80, we will boldly say, "I've still got work to do—*give me this mountain!*"

Today, defeat the Hivite giant. Don't pretend to be someone you are not. Don't wait for people or life to expose who you really are. Cross your Jordan. Take your mountain. Create your best life. This is not a season to wait. It is the season to possess. Mountains start from rocks. The rock of Jesus was designed to help you take mountains (sports, entertainment, healthcare, law, Wall Street, fine arts, etc.) in society. To take kingdoms of this world and make them powerful kingdoms of our God—to bring people to a saving knowledge of who He is.

Caleb, at the age of 80, was a rock that screamed, "Give me this mountain!" He was not satisfied with retirement. He didn't want to push paper while the younger generation drove out giants. He wanted to be hands-on to obtain the dream others had stolen from him forty years before.

Set a Time

We need the favor of King Jesus to defeat the giant of procrastination that keeps our lives in waste places. Our gift was designed to make room before great men and women—to stand before people of great influence, stature, wealth, and resources and to grant us boldness to leverage our platforms. But we must set a time.

In Nehemiah 2, we see an example of this. Nehemiah's city was in waste. The wall was broken down, and its gates destroyed by fire. Even though his destiny was in ruins and he was visibly preoccupied, Nehemiah went to work every single day.

> The king noticed Nehemiah's sad countenance and said, "What is it you want?" Then I prayed to the God of heaven, and I answered the king, "If it pleases the king and if your servant has found favor in his sight, let him send me to the city in Judah where my ancestors are buried so that I can rebuild it." Then the king, with the queen sitting beside him, asked me, "How long will your journey take, and when will you get back?" It pleased the king to send me; so I set a time. (Nehemiah 2:4-6 NIV)

Set a time today.

If you procrastinate, do so intentionally. Carve out blocks of time to work on the dreams in your heart. We must set a time to fight the giant of procrastination and pleasure. Nehemiah "set a time" because we cannot build without setting deadlines and eliminating time-wasters. Tell yourself:

- This is the time I will write book chapters.
- This is the time I will spend time with God.
- This is the time I will get up to read, write, study, or exercise.

We kill the giant of procrastination by setting a time.

CHAPTER 9

THE GIANT OF FOLLY

Jebusites: Threshers. Suppression of spiritual authority and potential in others. Legalism.

Have you ever had a dream you weren't ready to work for or craved something you hadn't earned yet? A credit card with a 20k limit? A million-dollar home? A brand-new Porsche?

When I was younger, I wanted everything that "successful" pastors and business owners had. But I was unwilling to pay the price in hard work, sweat, and tears— for my *own* anointing—to get it. The insatiable need to have more has penetrated our culture to the extent we get angry at people who have what we want. When we don't get what is in our heart, a sense of resignation can follow where we forsake morals, principles, and the Word of God to engage in something called folly.

King Solomon wrote, "As dead flies cause even a bottle of perfume to stink, so a little foolishness spoils great wisdom and honor" (Ecclesiastes 10:1 NLT).

Folly, defined as "a lack of good sense, or foresight; a foolish action, mistake, rashness, or senseless behavior" (*The Free Dictionary*), has destroyed humanity more than cigarettes, alcohol, drugs, heart disease, and cancer. Just a little folly can become a big giant in your life. It spoils any wisdom and honor you have built. It will rot—send a vile smell—in your leadership, dreams, and anointing. It will make you feel foolish, disqualified—unworthy of the call on your life.

King David participated in folly in 1 Chronicles 21:1-8 by taking an ill-advised census in battle. God was displeased. His commander-in-chief, Joab, tried to discourage the king and asked "Why do you want to do such a thing? No matter how many we have, God will multiply the troops a hundred times over!" But David overruled Joab. He ordered the count of non-disabled men who could fight. By the time he realized his sin of unbelief, it was too late.

Satan tempts you to distrust God. In Matthew 4, Satan told a fasting and hungry Jesus three things in the wilderness:

- "Make these stones bread."
- "Throw yourself from this cliff. You have been fasting forty days now. Your anointing should make you invincible. God will bear you up lest you dash your foot against a stone."
- "Bow down before me, and I will give you all the kingdoms of the earth."

Satan offered Jesus an ill-advised meal. A crown without a cross. A dare to test God and end his life prematurely. Satan comes to kill, steal, and destroy your anointing—to seduce you into folly or senseless decisions. To steal your appetite from the things of God to the things of this world. To kill your dreams or your calling before they are fulfilled. To destroy your allegiance and trust in God. To offer you a gospel without a cross, price, or death to self. To fix your mind on carnal, fading, and temporary things—present circumstances, pandemics, and giants. But don't fall for it. If you do, repent. Ask God to restore your trust in Him.

No Restoration, No Reconciliation

Eventually, David repented, but not before it cost seventy thousand men their lives. God gave him a choice of three years of famine, three months of being overtaken by his enemies, or three days of the delay of his dream by plagues ravaging his kingdom. David chose the penalty of plagues and said, "I'm in a desperate situation!" David replied to his seer Gad, "But let me fall into the hands of the Lord, for his mercy is very great. Do not let me fall into human hands" (1 Chronicles 21:13 NLT).

In Samuel's account, David refused to exacerbate his sin by repenting without cost. When David saw the angel, he said to the Lord,

"I am the one who has sinned and done wrong! But these people are as innocent as sheep—what have they done? Let your anger fall against me and my family." That day Gad came to David and said to him, "Go up and build an altar to the Lord on the threshing floor of *Araunah the Jebusite*." So David went up to do what the Lord had commanded him. When Araunah saw the king and his men coming toward him, he came and bowed before the king with his face to the ground. "Why have you come, my lord the king?" Araunah asked. David replied, "I have come to buy your threshing floor and to build an altar to the Lord there, so that he will stop the plague." *"Take it, my lord the king, and use it as you wish,"* Araunah said to David. "Here are oxen for the burnt offering, and you can use the threshing boards and ox yokes for wood to build a fire on the altar. *I will give it all to you*, Your Majesty, and may the Lord your God accept your sacrifice." But the king replied to Araunah, No, I insist on buying it, *for I will not present burnt offerings to the Lord my God that have cost me nothing."* So David paid him fifty pieces of silver for the threshing floor and the oxen. (2 Samuel 24:17-24 NLT, emphasis added)

Sacrifice always costs us something.

But the Jebusite giant said to David, "You don't have to pay for what you did. You don't have to sacrifice anything—or give up what you have. Your position insulates you from this sin. I can make you feel better with a false sense of righteousness—without true repentance or change. God owes you. He knows you were underprivileged or passed over. Not the first choice. You don't need to bear this cross or face this giant in your life. Take whatever you need to achieve what you want."

That's what Satan does.

He tells us that we don't have to change or be different in our generation. He offers shallow apologies and fake altar calls. But to avert the plague in David's life, created by reliance on human resources, God required a sacrifice. God always wants what we love.

David was willing to pay full price for something that was depreciated and used. In those estranged relationships in your life, are you willing to pay full price—*whatever it takes to see your family or friendships restored?* What is the cost of your repentance (*e.g.*, your fasting, worship, and prayer time)? What is the cost of your family reconciling? Your spouse or children forgiving you? Your career reviving? What are you willing to sacrifice or give up to salvage what's wrong in your life? One of our pastors Derek Golding once told me in the darkest season of my life, "Ed, the depth of our repentance is the depth of our deliverance."

The Jebusite giant makes a concerted effort to sugarcoat our repentance. To prevent us from growing taller. This giant stunts our growth. Keeps us stagnant. Makes us feel insignificant or ashamed when we try to walk in our own anointing. It tramples, treads, humiliates, or stomps us at our weakest point. It pacifies us and offers cheap sacrifice. It mocks our authority. We see King David, in 2 Samuel 5:6, facing this giant. "David then led his men to Jerusalem to fight against the Jebusites, the original inhabitants of the land who were living there. The Jebusites taunted David, saying, 'You'll never get in here! Even the blind and lame could keep you out!'" (NLT).

The Jebusite wants to crush your dream of truly being king—to take your throne and authority away.

I recently talked to a couple estranged from their adult children and grandchildren. It's been hard for them. I encouraged them to keep reaching, to keep uncovering and unpacking the offenses that led to the separation. Our kids need it more than we can imagine. Even when we are good providers and lay a good foundation of faith for our children, there are still unsaid, unresolved things in their lives. How do you determine if your kids still need to hear things from you? *Just think of the things you never heard from your parents.* This couple was raised in a generation when "I'm sorry" was never said to them, or it was said with only a handshake. They were transparent that apologizing was hard for them—especially when they felt they were right.

I commended them for the bravery of being transparent and said, "That's so awesome you can identify that. My parents were the same. But we get to make a change in our generation. We get to fill the holes or gaps left by our parents—with our children. If we think about the things that we still needed to hear from our parents, we will understand what our kids need to hear from us."

No matter what the age, sons and daughters still need to hear apologies from their parents. How we parent our children affect how they will eventually parent their own.

In those broken relationships, are you willing to say, "I was wrong? I crossed my boundaries. I tried to control you. That should have never happened. Will you ever forgive me?" Instead of "I'm sorry if I hurt or offended you," acknowledge we did hurt them. We can either pay the full cost of restoration or let the Jebusite giant influence us to seek a reconciliation without cost. Confronting pain in our children always cost us something.

The Child in You

In Matthew 18:1-4, the disciples asked Jesus, "'Who is greatest in the Kingdom of Heaven?' Jesus called a little child to him and put the child among them. Then he said, 'I tell you the truth, *unless you turn from your sins and become like little children*, you will never get into the Kingdom of Heaven. So anyone who becomes *as humble as this little child* is the greatest in the Kingdom of Heaven'" (NLT, emphasis added).

Why are we at our greatest when we are like little children? For three reasons:

I. Children forgive—they love, trust, and say "I'm sorry."

Whether you have children, work with them, or remember your childhood, you know what this means. We cannot see God transform our relationships until we repent and improve how we apologize to people.

In his book *Peacemaking for Families*, Ken Sande addresses seven key points of confession:

1. Confess to everyone involved. Confess to God, spouse, children, the person you hurt or offended.
2. Avoid the words: "if," "but," or "maybe." Don't minimize guilt. When you want to apologize and use a comma, put a period, and delete the rest of the sentence.
3. Admit specifically. Admit your heart condition and action (*e.g.*, "I spoke in anger because of my pride." Not, "I spoke in anger because you upset me.")
4. Apologize. Express sorrow for what you have done.
5. Accept consequences. I will buy another one. I will add 20 percent to it (Levitical law.)
6. Alter behavior. Say, "With the Lord's help, I'll do better."
7. Ask for forgiveness. Often, we don't get here. We just say, "sorry." But asking requires humility. It says you have something I need that I cannot give myself. Don't just be "sorry." Work on your apology language and approach. Practice reconciliation by paying the cost—the transaction to get there.

II. Children play—rehearsing their dream now as if it already existed.

As children, we dressed up and played house, doctor, fireman, cops, emulated actors, singers, and sports athletes. But when we grew up, society told us our dreams were not reality. Most of us believed it. Therefore, we were robbed of the life we imagined.

We worked hard to create a life we didn't love and wasted valuable years. But God will restore them. He will release your supernatural power to dream again.

III. Children imagine—believing they can be anything their mother or father says.

A child's imagination can live in the worst of circumstances and still find something to do or play. They don't need a real plane. Gravity does not deter them. They stretch their arms out and fly where they are. Children can commit the worst sin and still not lose the faith of their parents. But as adults, we condemn each other after one mistake. Thank God, our Heavenly Father, is not like our earthly father.

I heard a quote recently, "If airlines had a 90% success rate, we wouldn't fly." In other words, if while making an online airline reservation there was a disclaimer at the bottom of the webpage that said, "XYZ Airlines cannot guarantee you will make it to your final destination. There is a 10% chance your plane will crash," we would not fly. But imagine if a lawyer had a 90% success rate in hearings. A basketball player had a 90% free throw percentage rate. A quarterback had a 90% completion percentage in a game. They would be considered highly successful. But if an airline had the *same* success rate, they would not. It would deprive millions of taking off. We would not fly and see new places.

Often, we remain grounded in life. We refuse to fly—take a risk or try something new—unless there is a 100% guarantee we will succeed and not fail. We fail our generation, family, and workplace by refusing to confront this giant. We do our generation a disservice by remaining precisely like those who preceded us.

What's Stopping You from Flying?

As giant killers, we have the DNA to defy gravity—to defy odds. To be great at what we do, in spite of what we've done. To be remarkable. To do what people say we cannot do. But to have a vision, we must first have an imagination—a flight plan—so we can fly. Despite where sin has tried to ground or isolate us, our best life is waiting for us to come out and play (to work out the details).

People will hate you for being what they are not—for having the audacity to pursue your dreams when they didn't pursue theirs. When David came to confront Goliath, Eliab, the oldest brother who was passed over as king, was furious. Scripture records, "But when David's oldest brother, Eliab, heard David talking to the men, he was angry. 'What are you doing around here anyway?' he demanded. 'What about those few sheep you're supposed to be taking care of? I know about your pride and deceit. You just want to see the battle!'" (1 Samuel 17:28 NLT).

Eliab insulted David's anointing, by reminding him he was only a shepherd boy. He tried to trample his anointing and dreams and make him feel small. Later when David was on the run from death threats by King Saul, he lamented, "And I am this day weak, though anointed [but not crowned] king?" (2 Samuel 3:39 AMPC).

In what are you anointed by God, but not yet crowned or recognized by men, to do?

People will hate you for doing what they are afraid to do. They will remind you of your past or present. But God reminds us of our potential. That we have a right to royalty. We are children of the King, and the glory given to Jesus is ours (John 17:22).

When Jesus went to the cross, He replaced our physical lineage with His royal bloodline. He resurrected our spiritual authority that was destroyed in the Garden of Eden by sin. Over two thousand years later, God still operates by "death and resurrection." For the rest of your life, the death of all opposed to His nature in us is required (Hebrews 4:12).

Why? Because you will never experience resurrection without it. If your old life keeps hanging on the cross, prolonging death, you cannot bury it and rise to a new life. Once you defeat what has tried to kill you—once it drowns—it will never have power over you again. As we die to our relationship with sin, rituals of the past will stop breathing and God will breathe new life in us. Remember,

God is jealous. His name is Redeemer, Provider, Way Maker, Healer, Deliverer, Wonderful Counselor, and Prince of Peace. But according to Exodus 34:11, His name is also "Jealous." He is jealous for you and me. He said, "You will have no idols before me." He gave the Israelites a swift command to rid all giants before they became snares for them.

Dealing with Giants

Specifically, in Deuteronomy 7:2-5, the Lord gave ten commands for dealing with giants in the land:

1. You must destroy them.
2. You shall make no covenant with them.
3. You shall not show mercy to them.
4. You shall not make marriages with them.
5. You shall not give your children to them.
6. You shall break down their altars.
7. You shall dash in pieces their pillars.
8. You shall hew down their idols.
9. You shall burn their graven images with fire.
10. You shall not worship their gods.

If God's people obeyed Him, He promised:

- I will keep my covenant of unfailing love with you.
- I will love you and bless you and give you many children.
- I will give fertility to your land and your animals.

- You will have abundant harvests—of grain, new wine, and olive oil, and great herds of cattle, sheep, and goats.
- You will be blessed above all nations of the earth.
- No one will be childless.
- I will protect you from all sickness.
- I will not let you suffer from the terrible diseases that inflict your enemies. (Deuteronomy 7: 12-15)

The price for this promise was to face and destroy their giants.

In Genesis 23:7-20, Abraham bought the first property in Canaan, a tomb from the Hittites, after his wife died: "Then Abraham bowed low before the Hittites and said, 'Since you are willing to help me in this way, be so kind as to ask Ephron son of Zohar to let me buy his cave at Machpelah, down at the end of his field. I will pay the full price in the presence of witnesses, so I will have a permanent burial place for my family.'"

There is always a price to bury what is dead (or not working) in your life.

In the passage above, the enemy kept saying, "Bury your dead for free." The Hittite giant tried to give Abraham the burial site without price, but Abraham refused to accept it. He wanted to pay the full cost. He did not make a treaty with fear. He refused to let the enemy hold a transaction without charge over his head.

Often, we make agreements and allow giants to state, "I gave you this blessing—this car, job, contract, business,

179

etc.—so you should do whatever I say." We make transactions that cost us nothing now but leverage everything we love later. Abraham needed this transaction at the point of his greatest need. But he refused to bend his principles. He refused to agree with giants to get it done.

Everything free is not good for you. Don't make agreements you will regret later.

Don't Be Impulsive

King Solomon wrote, "Don't trap yourself by making a rash promise to God and only later counting the cost" (Proverbs 20:25 NLT).

Sometimes we make impulsive vows we cannot complete. We make uncalculated decisions we have not thought through. We want to help everyone and fix what is broken in the lives of people. We want to lead where there is no leadership. The truth is we are good at it. But just because we can meet needs, doesn't mean we should meet *every* need. One of my writing mentors once heard her pastor say, "A need doesn't always mean a call." Because anything hasty is of the enemy. Don't miss what God is trying to do in this season of your life. Don't forsake God's best for a temporary fix. When He goes before you, He sees things you cannot see. Trust Him.

When making vows, we should decide:

- Do I have what it takes to see it through—to finish building it?

- Do I have to give up anything to mentor, be in the relationship, or lay my life down for it?
- What will it cost me?

Jesus, before the nails—before the shame, betrayal, and weight of the world's sin was placed on Him—counted the cost. He did not make an impulsive vow. In the Garden of Gethsemane, as great drops of blood and sweat fell from His brow, and His disciples slept, He said, "My Father, if it is possible, let this cup pass from me." Then, under cover of night, Jesus faced the first act of violence by a disciple, a kiss by Judas (Luke 22:48-52).

But Jesus remembered His vow, the vow to die and become a ransom for many. Therefore, He was able to die to this moment. On the night His betrayal was in progress, He only thought of you and me. He said, "Don't forget what I did on the cross. Don't forget the sacrifice I gave so you could live. Don't forget how I became poor—gave up royalty so you could be rich. How I became filthy rags, so you could be the righteousness of God in Christ Jesus." He wanted to die for us. And somehow, on that rugged cross, convulsing and in agony—when He couldn't breathe—He remembered His vow. He saw us and made the vows we couldn't keep.

Overcoming Betrayal

One of our pastors, Samuel Carter, once said: "We are all betrayers."

Betrayal is something birthed in secret conspiracy. It can be fatal. If you don't get healed from what you did, or what people did to you, it will try to kill you.

In Genesis 45, Joseph told his estranged brothers that God used all the betrayal, jealously, and accusation he suffered to save many lives by a great deliverance. He finally matured into a man that embraced not only his destiny but everything he went through to get there. Growing up, his brothers hated him. Mocked him. Tried to kill him. They didn't want him in their lives. Now, in a famine, they needed him more than ever.

Maybe you've lived most of your life without God. In stark opposition to Him. You didn't desire Him or His dreams for you. But whether in famine, recession, or pandemic, Jesus is the lost brother in our lives. All the shame, betrayal, and rejection by you and me couldn't stop Him for coming to save us.

Jesus died to save your life, *not end it*. Don't quit. Don't throw in the towel. Live and declare the works of the Lord. Take your position as a giant killer in your generation. He loved you when He still knew you were a betrayer— that's the love of a father. But grace and forgiveness are not cheap. Jesus gave up something comfortable for you. It cost God the blood of His dear son, and it will cost you something. Repentance is not to be taken lightly.

You must give up something comfortable to achieve your dreams. You must give up something that feels good, to gain something that will *"be good"* for the rest of your life. You must give up your wilderness, to get a Promised

Land. Give up your fear, to kill a giant. Give up unforgive-ness, to get rid of your torment. It's the law of exchange.

Stay alive.

We have all sinned and fallen short of the glory of God. But Jesus—our giant killer—died to heal every heart deceived by a kiss (John 6:70).

CHAPTER 10

OUR FAMILY HISTORY

Many times, we view the things hanging from our family tree as harmless. Grandma reading weekly horoscopes. Dad's anger, foul mouth, drinking, or porn addiction. Mom's loose ways, manipulation, or multiple marriages. Parents constantly controlling, berating, or putting us down.

We make statements like: "Well, that's just the way I am." "I am angry because my mom or dad was angry." "I never had an opinion, so my kids won't." "My parents never apologized to me, so I don't apologize to them." "What I say goes." "This is how we raise kids." "Marriages don't work in our family—divorces do." "This is how we have always fought or communicated." "This is how my father and mother were—this is how I will be."

But God said don't leave any giants alive in your family lineage—destroy them all.

We find the command in Deuteronomy 20: "However, in the cities of the nations the Lord your God is giving you as an inheritance, do not leave alive *anything that breathes*. Completely destroy them—the Hittites, Amorites, Canaanites, Perizzites, Hivites and Jebusites—as the

Lord your God has commanded you. Otherwise, they will teach you to follow all the detestable things they do in worshiping their gods, and you will sin against the Lord your God" (v. 16 NIV, emphasis added).

That term, "Don't leave alive anything that breathes" refers to the Hebrew term of "the irrevocable giving over of things or persons to the Lord, by totally destroying them" (Deut. 20:16 Footnotes NIV). God said, destroy every habit. Every critical voice. Every generational pattern. Every streak of anger. Every residue of lust. Why? Because the giants, or habits, we (or our parents) do not destroy can grow up in our generation. Therefore, we must identify and kill them. The giants that Joshua's parents didn't confront were still there forty years later.

Bad History

My wife and I share not only our name, lifestyles, and traditions, but our genes with our three kids. Through genetic makeup, we can pass the natural beauty of our looks, hair color and type, unique facial features (*e.g.*, eyelashes, nose size), athletic prowess, and even metabolism to our children. Just pass a picture around of your kids or yourself to relatives, and you might hear someone say, "Oh, your children look just like you."

But the risk for disease can also stem from past generations. Recently, I went to the doctor because my blood pressure was high on a dentist visit. My physician began to ask me if my father or mother had any illnesses, and then recorded what I told them in my medical record.

Why? There is a good reason why doctors ask about our family history of illnesses.

According to the article, "Understanding Genetics: A New York, Mid-Atlantic Guide for Patients and Health Professionals," published by the Genetic Alliance, experts say: "Family history might be one of the strongest influences on your risk of developing heart disease, stroke, diabetes, or cancer ... Even though you cannot change your genetic makeup, knowing your family history can help you reduce your risk of developing health problems."

The giant the Israelites had to defeat in Canaan was bad family history.

After the Israelites entered the Promised Land, Joshua gave this powerful charge to the next generation:

> "Now fear the Lord and serve Him with all faithfulness. *Throw away* the gods your ancestors worshiped beyond the Euphrates River and in Egypt and serve the Lord. But if serving the Lord seems undesirable to you, then choose for yourselves this day whom you will serve, whether the gods your ancestors served beyond the Euphrates, or the gods of the Amorites, in whose land you are living. *But as for me and my household, we will serve the Lord.*" (Joshua 24:14-15 NIV, emphasis added)

Our family history is stronger than we think.

We are always making history. We are always leaving something behind. We cannot erase bad family history. We can only repeat or rewrite it.

Our decisions shape the next generation.

We can serve the seven giants—fear, dissatisfaction, pride, addiction, laziness, procrastination, or sin—the gods our ancestors served, or we can serve the Lord. We decide what family patterns cross over to the next generation in our lifetime. We determine the fruit that hangs or continues to grow from our family tree.

Just as doctors can link disease to heredity, present behavior can also be traced to family history. Asking your parents or family members about family history of marriages, divorces (*e.g.*, "Why didn't you and Dad work out?"), parenting, educational background, financial decisions, business, ministry, etc. can help us hold conversations instead of grudges, pain, and resentment. It can help reduce our risk of reproducing the same poor habits or trends in our lifetime.

Too often, people want conversations that feel, but not *reveal* good. But it's the unsaid things that speak the loudest in our lives. Don't underestimate the power of family history. Don't participate in the coverup of pain that has silenced previous generations. God listens to His children, no matter what age they are.

More than ever, I realize the responsibility I have to my adult children to excavate unresolved hurts, wounds, and embarrassments I caused when they were growing up, so they won't carry those things in life. We won't be perfect parents. Neither will they. But we can still kill the giants—the triggers that speak into their lives through us. If we don't kill Goliath—unresolved pain that grew—that same giant will attack our children with the memory of pain, or repeated behaviors in their adult life.

Anne Lamont once wrote this: "You own everything that happened to you. Tell your stories. If people wanted you to write warmly about them, they should have behaved better."

Tell your story to your spouse and kids. Your story is their story. They have been living it for years. Whether great memories or bad experiences, ask your parents or other relatives about lost relationships. Lessons learned. Mistakes made. Betrayals suffered. Redemption gained. Sins overcome. Unresolved abandonment issues.

We can't underestimate how our mothers and fathers lived (or how their parents' influence crept into their own dreams and destiny). We owe it to the next generation to talk to our parents and children about our family history— the good and the bad. There could have been cancer in both someone's body and marriage. Your parents could have struggled saying, "I'm sorry," because they never heard their parents say it. Your single mom could have stopped parenting you at some point because she had no example or point of reference. Perhaps she was abandoned by her mom too. Your father could have been a rolling stone because his father was one.

Physical descent from your family doesn't guarantee you will be just like them. Not all family history is bad and needing to be changed—just the diseased, poor behaviors that have passed through. Don't be a one hit wonder. David killed Goliath but still fell into adultery. You can win today and still lose tomorrow. Being a giant killer is to kill all the giants that occupy your space. Your real estate. Thought-life. Eyesight. Habits. Entertainment. Lifestyle. Your generation. If your parents were absent, grumbling, complaining, or fearful people, you don't have to transmit that to the next generation. You can change. Likewise, if they were solid, faithful men and women—successful and sold out for God—but you live in disobedience to Him, you will transmit that to your children.

Jesus did not choose family at the expense of His relationship with God.

In Matthew 10:34-37, He drew a line in our ancestry and said,

> Don't imagine that I came to bring peace to the earth! I came not to bring peace, but a sword. I have come to set a man against his father, a daughter against her mother, and a daughter-in-law against her mother-in-law. Your enemies will be right in your own household! If you love your father or mother more than you love me, you are not worthy of being mine; or if you love your son or daughter more than me, you are not worthy of being mine. (NLT)

This was not a command to sever ties with family. To dishonor our parents or in-laws. To not do good or help provide for them when it is in the power of our hands to do so. (See 1 Timothy 5:8) Jesus simply said you must draw the line of allegiance in your family tree.

It's either them or Me. Their ways or My ways. Their nature or Mine. Either you love them or love Me. Maybe you ask, can't I love both? Yes. But we must love Jesus more than anything else—pleasing Him, not people.

Don't ignore family history. Remember the blessings. Remember the patterns and curses. Uncover the risks of perpetuating unhealthy, diseased behavior to the next generation. Don't let these giants live another day. Drown them. Declare to every single one you see today, "I will see them no more."

I tried to give my kids what I didn't get growing up, but definitely missed the mark in some significant areas of their lives. As a father, I used to rely on saying, "Well, I was a good provider" or "I did the best I could." But we are supposed to provide. Parents who throw money at deficiencies in relationships with their children rarely succeed. Money never fills the holes we leave in our children's lives.

Jesus described this relationship in Matthew 15:8-9: "These people honor me with their lips, but their hearts are far from me. They worship me in vain; their teachings are merely human rules" (NIV).

Have you ever felt like that?

Had rules, but no relationship?

Unfortunately, no one is given a GPA in the school of parenting. We do the best we know how. But as we identify patterns of passing on to our children the bad things we received from our parents, we have to expose and kill every giant.

We can't just improve our salary and bottom-line profits. We must improve ourselves. This version of me must be better than yesterday's. As much as we work on our credit history, we must also work on our family history. What is your family history "credit" score? How many derogatory marks have you ignored?

Regardless of the past—good or bad—your family history is still being written by you. The next chapters belong to us.

Don't Leave Giants for Your Kids

The apostle Paul wrote, "So put to death the sinful, earthly things lurking within you. Have nothing to do with sexual immorality, impurity, lust, and evil desires. Don't be greedy, for a greedy person is an idolater, worshiping the things of this world. Because of these sins, the anger of God is coming" (Colossians 3:5-6 NLT).

God's standard for our lives is to kill every habit that sins—every hint of immorality, disobedience, bad tradition—no matter how it came into our lives.

Paul wrote there should not be any hint of sexual immorality. No indecent jokes. No foolish, sinful, silly, and corrupt talk. No coarse jesting. No idols. Idolatry can be categorized as pride, sexual sin, deifying self or something above God. It is fatal. God told the Israelites if they aroused His anger with these sins, they would quickly perish from the land He promised them. Yet there was hope. Deuteronomy 4:29-31 declares, "But from there you will search again for the Lord your God. And if you search for him with all your heart and soul, you will find him. In the distant future, when you are suffering all these things, you will finally return to the Lord your God and listen to what he tells you. For the Lord your God is a merciful God; he will not abandon you or destroy you or forget the solemn covenant he made with your ancestors" (NLT).

God wants everything. Everything that drives us away from Him. Everything that supplants His throne in our lives. Everything that worships what is fashionable or trendy because everyone else is doing it. We can't leave our giants to our children or pass on the things we made harmful covenants with. We can't give them our lemons— the things and people we have become bitter or angry in life over. King David wrote, "I will lead a life of integrity in my own home. I will refuse to look at anything vile and vulgar" (Psalm 101:2-3 NLT).

Beware of vile things in your family lineage or household. Don't approve of vulgar things detested by God. Live better. Love better. Dream better. Think better. Mother and father better. Act better. Don't pass off your parenting style as "No one is perfect." This isn't about perfection. It's about killing off the many giants in our lifetime, so they don't live in the next generation. The more giants we slay, the less our children may have to face.

Every seed we birth will face a giant. If we live in chaos, disorganization, or mess, our children may live in it. If we live in anger and bitterness, our children may struggle with it. If we live in promiscuity or have children out of wedlock, our children may continue that lifestyle in their generation.

The Lord told Moses, "I lavish unfailing love to a thousand generations. I forgive iniquity, rebellion, and sin. But I do not excuse the guilty. *I lay the sins of the parents upon their children and grandchildren; the entire family is affected*—even children in the third and fourth generations" (Exodus 34:7 NLT, emphasis added).

How does God punish the guilty for unaddressed sin? Through their children. *The cost of the sin we don't bring to Jesus is our son or daughter.* Generational curses are the result of unaddressed giants—open doors and unresolved sin in our parent's bloodline. It will be our children's giant until we cut its head off.

Our Weaknesses Become Our Giants

We see an example of this in Genesis 9:18-27:

The sons of Noah who came out of the boat with their father were Shem, Ham, and Japheth. From these three sons of Noah came all the people who now populate the earth. After the flood, Noah began to cultivate the ground, and he planted a vineyard. One day he drank some wine he had made, and he became drunk and lay naked inside his tent. Ham, the father of Canaan, saw that his father was naked and went outside and told his brothers. Then Shem and Japheth took a robe, held it over their shoulders, and backed into the tent to cover their father. As they did this, they looked the other way so they would not see him naked. When Noah woke up from his stupor, he learned what Ham, his youngest son, had done. Then he cursed *Canaan, the son of Ham*: "May Canaan be cursed! May he be the lowest of servants to his relatives." Then Noah said, "May the Lord, the God of Shem, be blessed, and may Canaan be his servant! May God expand the territory of Japheth! May Japheth share the prosperity of Shem, and *may Canaan be his servant.*" (NLT, emphasis added)

After building a great ark and surviving the flood, Noah got drunk. His younger, immature son Ham exposed his nakedness. His older, mature sons Shem and Japheth covered it. Verse 23 says, "They looked the other way so they wouldn't see him naked." A curse fell on Ham's lineage, and they were all put under the feet of Shem and Japheth because Ham did not cover his father's weaknesses, he exposed them. Giants expose what is in our heart. Ham's descendants later became the Canaanite giants.

Genesis 10 records:

- "This is the account of the families of Shem, Ham, and Japheth, the three sons of Noah. Many children were born to them after the great flood" (v.1).
- "The descendants of Ham were Cush, Mizraim, Put, and Canaan" (v.2).
- "Canaan's oldest son was Sidon, the ancestor of the Sidonians. Canaan was also the ancestor of the Hittites, Jebusites, Amorites, Girgashites, Hivites, Arkites, Sinites, Arvadites, Zemarites, and Hamathites. The Canaanite clans eventually spread out, and the territory of Canaan extended from Sidon in the north to Gerar and Gaza in the south, and east as far as Sodom, Gomorrah, Admah, and Zeboiim, near Lasha. These were the descendants of Ham, identified by clan, language, territory, and national identity" (vv.15-20).
- "These are the clans that descended from Noah's sons, arranged by nation according to their lines of descent. All the nations of the earth descended from these clans after the great flood" (v. 32 NLT)

Notice, all of the nations the Israelites were commanded to uproot were descendants of Ham, the son who exposed Noah's nakedness in Genesis 9. We can learn lessons from this startling fact: The giants of Canaan the Israelites had to drive out to obtain their promise were of the same ancestry. They were of the same family of Noah and his sons who survived the flood.

Canaan was a Hamite or son of Ham. Abraham was a Semite or son of Shem, brother of Ham. From one brother descended the Canaanites. From one brother descended Abraham to whom God promised in Genesis 17:5-7 to be a great nation.

The Israelites were the children of promise. But they had some bad cousins.

It was a family tree, like ours, tainted with sin. The Canaanites engaged in detestable practices: such as, sacrificing their sons and daughters in the fire, practicing sorcery, idolatry, and witchcraft, casting spells, and consulting the dead, among other things (See Deuteronomy 18). The command was swift: Destroy them all. This was not genocide. The conquest of Canaan was God's magnificent plan to ensure the next generation would not end up in a worse state than their predecessors.

God waited more than four centuries to bring judgment upon the inhabitants of Canaan. He told Abraham, "After four generations, your descendants will return here to this land, for the sins of the Amorites do not yet warrant their destruction" (Genesis 15:16 NLT).

God already saw the future defilement of the land He promised to His people. He waited until the sin, the size of giants in the land, had reached its full measure to prepare a people courageous, bold, and numerous enough to drive them out. But He was no respecter of persons. Whether it was giants in the land or His own people, He was territorial over the land He promised.

God told the Israelites:

You said your children would be carried off as plunder. Well, I will bring them safely into the land, and they will enjoy what you have despised. But as for you, you will drop dead in this wilderness. And your children will be like shepherds, wandering in the wilderness for forty years. In this way, they will pay for your faithlessness, until the last of you lies dead in the wilderness. Because your men explored the land for forty days, you must wander in the wilderness for forty years—a year for each day, suffering the consequences of your sins. Then you will discover what it is like to have me for an enemy." I, the Lord, have spoken! I will certainly do these things to every member of the community who has conspired against me. They will be destroyed here in this wilderness, and here they will die!" (Numbers 14:31-35 NLT)

Then God told Joshua, "I will give you every place where you set your foot, as I promised Moses" (Joshua 1:3 NIV). While grieving the death of his predecessor, God commanded Joshua and his generation to cross over the skeletons of their dead parents in the wilderness and storm the gates of their giants—their tainted cousins—to achieve their highest dreams. After Moses died, God buried the body. God wouldn't even allow the next generation to mourn at the gravesite of what was.

God told the Israelites they would die in the wilderness. For each day they explored the land in doubt, making excuses not to possess it, they would suffer and know what it was like to have God against them (Num. 14:26-35). Our children pay for our unfaithfulness. If we want our kids to have a better generation, we must confront the unaddressed things we did, which grew into giants in their lives. Why didn't God sentence the children in the wilderness with their parents? He wanted to give them a chance to do something their parents hadn't done before. To change their family history. To cut off grumbling and complaining. Adultery. Family dysfunction. Unfaithfulness. Sin and sexual things.

Don't underestimate family giants.

God didn't just randomly pick Canaan on the map. It was a land of giants promised to Abraham's bloodline when in Genesis 9:25-26, Noah declared on Ham's lineage, "May Canaan be cursed! May he be the lowest of servants to his relatives. ...May the Lord, the God of Shem, be blessed, and may Canaan be his servant!" (NLT). These giants—descendants of Ham—were destined to be under the feet of Shem's chosen bloodline, the Israelites.

Be the Best of Your Generation

Why would God command Abraham and his descendants to take land from their own relatives? Because we must defeat family giants related to a common ancestor. We are constantly taking territory possessed by something related to our past. Exchanging our physical lineage for our new one in Christ.

In some sense, the Israelites were fighting themselves. They were confronting the worst of their family history, which died in the wilderness, to become the best of their generation—a greater version than their predecessors—to possess all God planned for them. They were to destroy every bad living memory from the past. Everything their parents believed in that displeased God. Too often, we try to coexist with old habits, fears, traditions, cultural mindsets, failed marriages, and the sins of our fathers or ancestors.

My father was not around when I was young, he did not raise me. My only childhood memory of him was when he called one day to say he was going to pick me up and buy me a "coat." I remember being thrilled to see him. At the time, bomber jackets were trendy in school, so I wrapped up for a cold day of father-and-son time to drive to the store with him and buy the first gift or necessity he had ever given me. To my dismay, he walked me to the corner liquor store and brought me a "coke," not a "coat." I was crushed.

Recently, I asked him, "Dad, what happened between you and Mom? What kept you from being a part of my life growing up? It hurt not having you there."

That's when he told me, "Ed, I don't know if you are my son or not."

My first reaction was anger because for the thirty years he was in my adult life, he never mentioned it until I confronted him about his absence in my childhood. I also thought about responding with empathy, "Dad, that must have been hard, not knowing." That's when God revealed to me, "It is not your responsibility to counsel your own bad family history or cure your dad." Our job is to bring the pain of our past to the feet of Jesus. He is a Wonderful Counselor. Mighty God. Everlasting Father. Prince of Peace (Isaiah 9:6 NIV).

Confessing the Sins of Your Ancestors

In Nehemiah 9:2, the Israelites had just rebuilt the gates that had been destroyed and laid waste for generations: "On the twenty-fourth day of the same month, the Israelites gathered together, fasting and wearing sackcloth and putting dust on their heads. Those of Israelite descent had separated themselves from all foreigners. They stood in their places and confessed their sins and the sins of their ancestors" (NIV).

The Israelite's rebuilding of something their parents left in ruins sparked a revival of repentance.

When rebuilding, they confessed not only their sins, but the sins of the ancestors whose bad family history had imprinted their very lives. This leaves us with a startling fact: It's not enough to know our family history, we have to repent from it (especially if our parents won't or can't). We have to pray, "Lord, I repent for the sins of my mom or dad not providing for me. For them not taking accountability for their stark absence in my life. I repent for the sins of parents who were silent, critical, abusive—who did not listen to, or comfort me in known and unknown hurts, disappointments, and rejections. I repent for extending my ancestral anger, unforgiveness, indifference, or generational sins to my kids. For not validating their questions—their "whys" in life. For saying no without explanation. For loving with provision, but not with words, comfort, and understanding."

To identify with the sins of a parent, family, or race (*i.e.,* systemic racism, anger, pride, pornography, idols), and ask God to forgive unrepentant sin by previous generations—ancestors who took their sins stubbornly to the grave—breaks generational curses. It is also a mark of maturity. Repenting for the sins of our ancestors releases the blessing of God. Often in ancient times, God looked for the intercession of just one leader to spare countless deaths over a nation (i.e., Moses/Sodom, Jonah/Nineveh), and release the blessing of their forefathers.

Today, God is looking for you to confront the sin that previous generations ignored—to condemn past sin and the residue it leaves on present generations.

The apostle Paul wrote in Romans 8:28: "And we know that in all things God works for the good of those who love him, who have been called according to his purpose. For those God foreknew he also predestined to be conformed to the image of his Son, that he might be the firstborn among many brothers and sisters. And those he predestined, he also called; those he called, he also justified; those he justified, he also glorified (NIV).

People can't restore what they stole from you. Only God can.

When God justifies (and acquits) us, He hurls what has been done in the deepest parts of the sea—as if it never happened. (See Micah 7:19). When we repent, He makes things that hurt—that are wrong—right. And His justice will not fail us even when our parents do, even when *we* fail the next generation.

Regardless of who my earthly father is, I am loved by my Heavenly Father. When people reject you as their child, God won't. He chose you. Accepted you. Wanted you. When your mother or father forsook you, He took you as His own. Loved you with an everlasting love. When the human representatives of this earth fail, He is unfailing. He will make up for the parents who weren't there in your life. But you must bring those hurts to Him. Don't live with them another day or stuff them away in denial. Either you feel it now, or you (and someone you love) will feel it later. If you don't acknowledge the holes in your life, you will live with them for another decade. If you ignore the pain, Jesus cannot heal and make you whole.

I vowed when I had children of my own, I would try to give them everything my dad hadn't provided for me when I was growing up. But as a father, I too have fallen short. My kids can tell you stories of me hurting or disappointing them at some point—not giving them enough of what they needed.

Why? Because what happened in Canaan happens in every family. We all have sinned and fallen short of the glory of God. But thank goodness, our earthly father is not like our Heavenly Father. Unlike man, God carries His children all the way until they reach the fulfillment of their potential and destiny (Deuteronomy 1:29-31). He releases wisdom and words of encouragement until every giant keeping us out of the Promised Land dies. He doesn't quit on us. He doesn't diminish our hopes and dreams. He resurrects them. Don't think God will expect anything less from us in our generation. We cannot be exactly like our parents. We must be better. We must mimic the God we saw in them, but also tear down any strongholds they erected. We must teach our children and the next generation to do the same.

In Genesis 50:19-25, Joseph said to his brothers,

"Don't be afraid of me. Am I God, that I can punish you? You intended to harm me, but God intended it all for good. He brought me to this position so I could save the lives of many people. No, don't be afraid. I will continue to take care of you and your children." So he reassured them by speaking kindly to them. Joseph and his brothers and their families continued to live in Egypt. Joseph lived to the age of 110. He lived to see three generations of descendants of his son Ephraim, and he lived to see the birth of the children of Manasseh's son Makir, whom he claimed as his own. "Soon I will die," Joseph told his brothers, "but God will surely come to help you and lead you out of this land of Egypt. He will bring you back to the land he solemnly promised to give to Abraham, to Isaac, and to Jacob." Then Joseph made the sons of Israel swear an oath, and he said, "When God comes to help you and lead you back, you must take my bones with you." (NLT)

Joseph said, "Don't keep me buried in this temporary place of residence." Like Joseph and his family, we can live in a place of favor and comfort at the expense of God's best. Good is the enemy of His best. Passivity is the enemy to prosperity. Comfort is the enemy to change. Here, Joseph is a father to Pharaoh. His family and brothers have been given the best of all of Egypt to live in. But Egypt is not their home. There is a greater position. A greater place. A greater calling to respond to.

Comfort Zones Are Fatal

The people of Jonestown were comfortable. They became attached to Jones and each other despite the abuse. They had done some good together, which made them ignore the bad family history they experienced. They feared change. Feared to start over. Feared for their safety. So, they stayed in a bad relationship. It was a relationship that started with excitement, but quickly shifted to control and abuse. Most of the people in Jonestown were related, families following mothers, fathers, grandfathers, and relatives to their eventual deaths.

Too often, we reproduce fruit that fell from our family tree. We don't just learn our name or language from family. We learn behaviors. Habits. Faith. Respect. Love, forgiveness, and leadership styles.

At the age of six, the Jonestown Tragedy became a part of my bad family history. Many people have called it a mass suicide, but what happened first helps us understand what happened last. U.S. Congressman Leo Ryan did not drink poisoned Kool-Aid. He was gunned down and killed. Therefore, it is incomprehensible to believe that all 900 people were given a choice to live after his brutal assassination. To the contrary, they were given no alternative but to die. The biggest lie about Jonestown is that all the victims committed revolutionary suicide. The hysterics heard on the death tape are the screams and cries of people who did not want to die. It was not a solemn ritual. They were screaming for their lives.

In *The Black Hole of Guyana: The Untold Story of the Jonestown Massacre* (1985), John Judge writes:

Dr. [Leslie] Mootoo, the top Guyanese pathologist, was at Jonestown within hours after the massacre. Refusing the assistance of U.S. pathologists, he accompanied the teams that counted the dead, examined the bodies, and worked to identify the deceased. While the American press screamed about the "Kool-Aid Suicides," Dr. Mootoo was reaching a much different opinion ... Dr. Mootoo found fresh needle marks at the back of the left shoulder blades of 80-90% of the victims. Others had been shot or strangled. One survivor reported that those who resisted were forced by armed guards ... Chief Medical Examiner Mootoo's testimony to the Guyanese grand jury investigating Jonestown, led to their conclusion that all but three of the people were murdered by 'persons unknown.'

Today, 406 unidentifiable bodies rest in a mass grave at the Evergreen Cemetery in Oakland, California, in a plot purchased by the U.S. government when Evergreen agreed to allow the bodies to be interred there. On the plot, stands a memorial plaque with Jim Jones's name inscribed as if he was one of the victims. He was not. He is not even buried there. Further, according to 18 U.S.C. Sections 2381 and 2385, Jim Jones committed a federal offense by assassinating an elected member of the US Congress. It is incomprehensible that the plaque, which memorializes Congressman Leo Ryan and over 900 victims, includes the inscription of their murderer's name. This memorial perpetuates the lie that what happened in Jonestown was mass suicide and not premeditated murder.

Charles Krause, a *Washington Post* foreign correspondent, traveled with Congressman Leo Ryan and his entourage to visit Jonestown. He survived the ambush on the Port Kaituma airstrip by playing dead after being shot in the hip. On the 40th anniversary of the tragedy, he was asked by Caitlin Gibson of the *Washington Post*: "We now have generations of people who are too young to remember Jonestown, and are more familiar with derivative pop-culture references—like the phrase *"drink the Kool-Aid"*— than the facts of the tragedy itself. But even that phrase isn't true to what happened, right?

Krause replied, "Right. I remember very distinctly, about three weeks after all of it, I heard from the president of Kool-Aid—and I was afraid, you know, are we going to start with a lawsuit and all of this? But it was just a very nice note saying, 'Look, we just wanted you to know that as it turns out it wasn't Kool-Aid, but we understand that Kool-Aid is sort of generic for all kinds of flavored drinks, and we wish you well.' Apparently, it was Flavor Aid. But regardless, it was mixed with cyanide—and no, people didn't take it voluntarily. In fact, there is a recording that exists, and you can hear the people asking, "Why are we doing this—do we really have to do this?" And then they had men with guns. So they really didn't have much of a choice. And the children didn't have a choice."

In Jonestown, 305 children inherited the fatal decisions of their parents. Tragically, we can say, the children drank the poisonous thoughts their parents gave them. They gave the children their giants.

But Jesus took God's wrath from us. He came to defeat the giant of bad family history.

G.O.A.T.

Jesus was the world's greatest fighter—the greatest of all time. Yet He didn't lay a single hand on men. He spoiled principalities and powers—generational giants— by laying down His life. Then He raised it, with us, in great power. He pulled down strongholds and thought patterns and eliminated the trace of bad decisions, rendering our past powerless. Like Him, we are born from a lineage of giant killers.

Don't believe the lie of Goliath. He will bring condemnation that the wrath of God is coming, and we are too late. Doomed. Unforgivable. Irretrievably broken. But Jesus came to take that away too. When He looks at our lives and the sins we have committed, He is not short, deficient, or stuck with insufficient funds. He does not hold grudges. He has more than enough grace. More than enough mercy. More than enough forgiveness for you.

The apostle Paul wrote, "But because of his great love for us, God, who is rich in mercy, made us *alive* with Christ even when we were dead in transgressions—it is by grace you have been saved" (Ephesians 2:4 NIV, emphasis added).

How do we become alive with Christ? By closing the doors our fathers and mothers opened that we walked into. By putting to death sinful habits so that He can live. By refusing to drink the bad things people have given us and by strengthening the good things sown into our life.

In the Old Testament, some never entered into what God promised. Every tribe, every family in Israel was to possess territory. Every family had to face a giant: to dispossess and exterminate what stood in front of them. But some never entered into what God promised. Don't follow these footsteps. Just because we ignore Goliath doesn't mean he will shut up or go away. He will wait for our children and those we lead. He will disrupt our dreams with unaddressed habits grown into giants. But we live in the commanded and established promise of God upon our generation:

- "I will give you what is stronger and mightier than you."
- "I will make one of you into a thousand."
- "I will allow no man to do you wrong."
- "I will rebuke kings for your sake." (See 1 Chronicles 16:15-22).

Jesus is the Savior from the hand of every giant that hates us. Every sickness. Every disease. Every diagnosis. Every demon that screams at us—everything. He saves us to serve Him in the worst of circumstances. King David wrote, "And He saved them from the hand of him that hated them and redeemed them from the hand of the [Egyptian] enemy. And the waters covered their adversaries; not one of them was left" (Psalm 106:10-11 AMP).

Jesus said the world will hate us because we are different. Because we love and live for Him and stand up for what is right. We are unlike anything the world has ever seen. So, give Him everything. He bore our shame and guilt so the little boy or girl in us could be heard and healed.

CHAPTER 11

A CRITICAL SPIRIT

We've been talking about how to identify and drive out habits holding your dreams hostage—seven giants standing between you and Jericho. But this book is about more than giants. It is about you and the legacy you leave behind.

Be A Giant Killer was written to help restore family history by effectively producing giant killers that influence the next generation.

The "Joshua generation" that seized Jericho were born to complainers and murmurers, to families living outside of God's best, to a people who settled for mediocrity—first in Egypt, then in the wilderness. No one finished high school. No one had a degree. No one was a homeowner. No one left a point of reference for conquest or achieving dreams to the children born in the wilderness. They were slave-minded—children of stubborn, disobedient, ungrateful, and critical people.

Have you ever lived with someone like that—a pessimist—constantly negative—who always sees the worst in things?

When moving toward your dream or vision, there will always be people—with good or wrong intentions—saying, "You can't do this. You will lose. You cannot afford or finish school. You can't start a business. Plant a church. Succeed in that career or marriage. You won't take the city or go up and possess the land." These are people who would tolerate, rather than transform, an unfulfilled life.

The negative perception of things—how giants appear—how you appear to them—can sabotage your pursuit of destiny. Jesus said, "A kingdom divided by civil war will collapse. Similarly, a family splintered by feuding will fall apart. And if Satan is divided and fights against himself, how can he stand? He would never survive" (Mark 3:24-26 NLT).

One of my favorite quotes is by Winston Churchill, who once said, "You will never reach your destination if you stop and throw rocks at every dog that barks."

Dogs are distractions barking at you, pulling you away from your goals to silence them. Offense is inevitable, but feuds are fatal. If you, your family, team, or church are divided, you cannot stand or go very far. To advance, we must have hard and honest conversations. We must confront the system we want to change and eliminate critical spirits around us. The ten spies who saw themselves as grasshoppers—in comparison to giants—had not seen walled cities before. They were overwhelmed at the sight of giants, cities, and walls. They were critical. They forfeited their dream. Lost sight of God's power. Saw their enemies in comparison to themselves—instead of in contrast to God.

Fear produces a lie that God is incapable of overcoming your biggest giant.

We see an example of this in Numbers 11:1-6:

Soon the people began to complain about their hardship, and the Lord heard everything they said. Then the Lord's anger blazed against them, and he sent a fire to rage among them, and he destroyed some of the people in the outskirts of the camp. Then the people screamed to Moses for help, and when he prayed to the Lord, the fire stopped. After that, the area was known as Taberah (which means "the place of burning"), because fire from the Lord had burned among them there. Then the foreign rabble who were traveling with the Israelites began to crave the good things of Egypt. And the people of Israel also began to complain. "Oh, for some meat!" they exclaimed. "We remember the fish we used to eat for free in Egypt. And we had all the cucumbers, melons, leeks, onions, and garlic we wanted. But now our appetites are gone. All we ever see is this manna!" (NLT)

As giant killers, don't crave what is behind you. Don't hang around critics—people who make Egypt and giants look like something they're not. Don't be discouraged by individuals who have never taken a city. Never run a company. Never pioneered a thriving church. Never built a healthy marriage. Never raised successful children. Never owned real estate. Never made six figures or sustained a powerful brand. Don't let unqualified—critical naysayers tell you what you cannot do.

Eleanor Roosevelt once said, "Never let anyone tell you no, that does not have the power to say yes."

To be a giant killer, we must disempower critical spirits. We must realize critical spirits don't function off lies. They exist off something true, factual, and real. The foreigners in the above passage were dead right. They did have free meat, fish, cucumbers, melons, onions, and garlic in Egypt. But they were also enslaved in bondage. Because whenever you eat things for free, there is no freedom or autonomy. No promise fulfilled. You let people set your diet.

A critical spirit is deceptive. It makes you indecisive. It always opposes and ridicules the dream you are trying to build in life. In the book of Nehemiah, Sanballat and opponents came to fight, injure, cause confusion, and failure in the vision Nehemiah had undertaken.

Likewise, the construction of your dream will increase the noise of those who don't believe in you—critics that defy the completion of what is in your heart. But your dream will not be a myth or false idea. It will be a master-piece. Keep building it.

Three Things About a Critical Spirit

1. A critical spirit will keep you in a desert.

God will not tolerate a critical person—someone who can change their life but complains instead. A person who wants to eat for free and comes to the table to eat the Word of God, enjoy the cloud of His protection, and the miracles of His provision, but never lays down their life for it.

God could overcome Pharaoh with all of his chariots, oppression, and rule for 430 years—his hardened heart on ten separate occasions—but He could not overcome the critical and hardened hearts of Israel. So, God allowed the critical generation to stay in the wilderness until they died. Not only did they not go in, but He did not let them see the Promised Land. Critical spirits will keep you outside the wall of your dreams.

2. A critical spirit may exist in the gap between what you are getting and what you are expecting.

Why are they critical? Why do people fight? File frivolous lawsuits? Falsely accuse you? Try to get you fired or make you look bad in front of the boss? Why do people mock your dream, business, or calling and say it will not work? Somehow, they feel they did not get something owed to them in life. They are war-makers instead of peace-makers. (See James 4:1-3).

Whether you are the cause or not, a critical spirit will fight and feud from this origin of dissatisfaction. The book of James says, "You want what you don't have, so you scheme and kill to get it. You are jealous of what others have, but you can't get it, so you fight and wage war to take it away from them. Yet you don't have what you want because you don't ask God for it. And even when you ask, you don't get it because your motives are all wrong—you want only what will give you pleasure" (4:2-3 NLT).

In other words, if you fix your heart, you'll fix your asking. You will never obtain what you want by being envious or blaming others for what you don't have. The Israelites thought the longer they were in the wilderness, the Promised Land was a lie or in jeopardy. But our inheritance in Christ is incorruptible. It is reserved and laid up for us in a place where thieves cannot break-in—where moth cannot destroy. Your dream is safe. No thief can steal it. No rust can destroy it. The purses of heaven never get old (Luke 12:29-34; Matthew 6:20 NLT).

For every year the Israelites did not take possession of what God promised, it increased in value. In milk and honey. In houses and land. In commerce. God multiplied the fear of their footsteps. He took the wealth of giants and gave it to them.

Do you please God?

Do you love Him?

If so, He promises wisdom, knowledge, and joy. He commands the sinner to gather, heap up, and give to you (Ecclesiastes 2:26 NLT). The giants in Canaan were holding the Israelites' best life, best inheritance, and best family history hostage until they were ready to take it back.

Whether in heaven or on earth, Jesus is always preparing and constantly keeping something ready—something greater for us—"superabundantly, far over and above all that we [dare] ask or think [infinitely beyond our highest prayers, desires, thoughts, hopes, or dreams]" (Ephesians 3:20 AMPC). But a critical spirit will keep you disconnected from God's best.

3. A critical spirit must be cut off.

The apostle Paul wrote to the Colossians: "You were dead because of your sins and because your sinful nature was not yet cut away. Then God made you alive with Christ, for he forgave all our sins. He canceled the record of the charges against us and took it away by nailing it to the cross. In this way, he disarmed the spiritual rulers and authorities. He shamed them publicly by his victory over them on the cross" (Colossians 2:13-15 NLT).

Sometimes, we are connected—by blood—to sinful patterns. To grumbling and complaining ways. Still envious. Still angry. Messy. Selfish. Lustful. Greedy. We are still connected to the wrong things—wanting to go back to what we used to be.

But the apostle Paul urged us to put to death the earthly and unspiritual things lurking in our hearts and thoughts and have nothing to do with them (Colossians 3:5).

That word "lurking" means:

1. To lie in wait, as in ambush.
2. To move furtively; to sneak.
3. To exist unobserved or unsuspected.

That's what a critical spirit or sin does. It lurks. It lies in wait to contaminate your thoughts, decisions, words, and actions. It ambushes your highest dreams, hopes, and expectations by keeping you connected to the wrong thoughts. The wrong habits. The wrong television programs or movies. The wrong music. The wrong circle of friends. The wrong motives and discussions. The wrong and unhealthy fears. A critical spirit keeps you disconnected from God's best life for you.

Be Healed

After the Israelites left the place where their parents died, we read how the Lord dealt with any residue of bad habits left by their ancestors:

At that time the Lord told Joshua, "Make flint knives and circumcise this second generation of Israelites. So Joshua made flint knives and circumcised the entire male population of Israel at Gibeath-haaraloth. Joshua had to circumcise them because all the men who were old enough to fight in battle when they left Egypt had died in the wilderness. Those who left Egypt had all been circumcised, but none of those born after the Exodus, during the years in the wilderness, had been circumcised. The Israelites had traveled in the wilderness for forty years until all the men who were old enough to fight in battle when they left Egypt had died. For they had disobeyed the Lord, and the Lord vowed he would not let them enter the land he had sworn to give us—a land flowing with milk and honey. So Joshua circumcised their sons—*those who had grown up to take their fathers' places*—for they had not been circumcised on the way to the Promised Land. After all the males had been circumcised, they rested in the camp *until they were healed.* (Joshua 5:2-8 NLT, emphasis added)

As long as they did not cut away the flesh, their sons and daughters could not take the city. We can't get to where we want doing the wrong thing. We can't escape the painful decisions of our parents, still harboring them in our hearts, still reacting in response to unchanged behavior. If we can't do the right thing, we need to bring our hurts and disappointments to Jesus and let Him heal us. Your giants will still be there. Your parents may still be there. They can wait. You can't.

The Israelites had to be circumcised before they took Jericho. *They remained at the place they were injured until they were healed.* God is always concerned about your pain *more* than your promise. Your healing *more* than your accomplishments. Your address *more* than your destination. So don't move—be healed.

Let God redeem you from the things your predecessors have done. From their actions and inaction. Things that should have been done for you. He wants to cut away the things that hurt. Decisions that kept you in a wilderness of painful pasts, instead of a land of glorious future. Your parents may be dead or unwilling to change, but nothing prevents God, the Healer, from using you—healing and empowering you—to transform the next generation.

The Escape Plan

Wisdom comes when we become generational giant killers—when we dare confront the sinful areas of our lives that threaten our anointing, leadership, and destiny. The fear of the Lord—living in deep awareness of what God is displeased with and fleeing it—is the beginning of all wisdom. (See Proverbs 8:11-16 TPT).

God always gives us a way of escape.

To flee youthful lusts—things you indulged in or fell into easily early in your life, which are still trapping you—means *run*. Run before the thought becomes an action. Run while in the very act, while watching, while seeing where a certain road or behavior is leading. *Run!* Get out. God has set it up that the more we flee sin, the more He releases wisdom to save us. Making right decisions is a weapon against making bad ones. When we hate the sin in our life, we release the wisdom of God in our life.

Instead of living like a victim in your circumstance ("Lord take it away!"), why not thank Him for chiseling your heart? For revealing and refining your character? For making you a giant (fear, procrastination, addiction, or folly) killer?

Sin is a giant.

Psalm 105:19 says: "Until the time came to fulfill his dreams, the LORD tested Joseph's character."

You have never been closer to your dream than you are right now.

Maybe it feels afar off. That it will never happen. You don't deserve it. Maybe you keep getting angry. You feel too weak in character. You can forgive but can't forget. You keep relieving the same nightmare or making the same mistakes. You can't turn the corner in your gift. You are still deficient in certain areas of your life.

This is not the season to give up. This is the season to escape the person we were and become the person we always dreamed we'd be. The reward—riches of righteousness—for killing giants far exceeds the value of any paycheck, jewel, or six-figure income. (See Proverbs 8:14-21 TPT).

But before we can truly march on what God promised, we must cut away past failures. It's easy to feel we are still paying for what we did—for what happened to us. It's easy to drown your past in drugs, alcohol, or sex. To ignore what happened or silence it by climbing the corporate ladder of success or busyness. But only a relationship with a real Savior—a real Jesus, who has a real plan and purpose for your—life can rid or roll it away.

In Joshua 5, the next generation God was preparing to lead was different. They were giant killers. Born in the wilderness, they didn't see the miraculous signs and wonders God performed in Egypt against Pharaoh. They didn't see what the Lord did to the Egyptian soldiers, horses, and chariots—how He drowned them in the Red Sea and destroyed them beyond the point of recovery. They didn't know how the Lord cared for them in the wilderness supernaturally when they were children. They didn't see when God opened the earth in the Israelite camp at the rebellion and swallowed up critical people—Dathan and Abiram along with their households and tents—and every living thing that belonged to them.

Unfamiliar to previous moves of God, they were *marked* to exceed the obedience of the previous generation. There is a *mark* on your life too. Jesus said in Matthew 5:20: "But I warn you—unless your righteousness is better than the righteousness of the teachers of religious law and the Pharisees, you will never enter the Kingdom of Heaven!" (NLT).

We must be better.

Don't reject the call to take uncharted territory in your generation. There are doors to open. Doors to close. New rooms to unlock. Promises to possess. Giants to conquer. As we prepare to take the city, if we let Him, God will heal us. He will roll away the reproach and shame of our ancestral bloodline (Joshua 5:8). He will take away what our parents didn't or couldn't do for us—so we can be born again—to heal every bad thing or decision responsible for who we are today. He commands us to do the same for our children.

There is a destiny, purpose, and dream killer present in our lives today. It is called sin. But Jesus crucified it. He chose you and me—flawed and all—to *perfect* that which concerns us—to transform us into generational giant-killers (1 Corinthians 6:9-11).

CHAPTER 12

CONTAMINATED DREAMS

John and Wanda Crawford, two of the former members of my life group, taught a class at Melodyland Christian Center called "Wisdom is a Defense."

You will either learn wisdom—good sense—by instruction or by punishment. Wisdom is the *fruit* of instruction and correction you have received. Unfortunately, the Israelites refused to be corrected. They refused to pursue their calling because of fear. Therefore, they disqualified themselves.

Are you afraid to take risks? Make mistakes? Reluctant to pursue your dream because of giants?

My oldest son, Joshua, didn't have the high school basketball career he dreamed of. Overcoming some racial obstacles, he didn't start on varsity until his senior year. Nevertheless, Josh learned the lesson of hard work. In his last high school game, playing for the Troy High School Warriors (where he transferred) against eventual Division 1A champions, Temecula Valley, he closed with his best game of the year. He led the team with 17 points, 9 rebounds, 4 steals, 3 assists, and 1 block. He closed the year third overall in steals (61) in the Freeway League and led his team overall in steals, rebounds, and blocks. But after that playoff loss against Temecula, he came off the court in tears. He poured everything out. He knew it was over and was crushed with regret. I looked intently at him and told him, "Son, I am so proud of you. You played your heart out and have nothing to be ashamed of." That year, he hung up his basketball shoes and picked up his pencil to study another passion: art and animation.

The problem: Josh was behind other art students in skill because of years focusing on playing basketball and not drawing. He initially was accepted by Otis School of Art but had his heart set on attending Gnomon School of Visual Arts, which had rejected his application. But Josh was relentless. He took several six- week classes at Gnomon to improve his portfolio, gaining acceptance within the year. Josh's work ethic inspires me. He graduated as a 3D animator with a 4.0 GPA. He is a true example of using wisdom to slay giants—past regrets in life.

Regret is a thief. It robs us of time—and the power to make redemptive decisions.

Whether or not you have all the wisdom of King Solomon, you will make mistakes. Herbert V. Prochnow asserted, "The fellow who never makes a mistake takes his orders from one who does."

In the longest recorded sermon in the Bible, Moses preached his last message to the generation he failed to take into the Promised Land. Imprisoned by a life of regret and mistakes, he was a dead man walking. He would only see the Promise Land from a distance. He would not possess it. He was disqualified. He had lost the opportunity to face his giants. His time was up. He urged the next generation: "Live this—do this now! Don't miss it. Learn from my failures. Don't make the mistakes of your parents. They brought you out, but could not take you in. This is your hour. Go in. Do what we could not do. Defeat what we could not defeat. March on what we were afraid of."

Why? Because God never intended for experience to be our only teacher. Why does a man have to get into a fatal accident, which destroys a family, to realize he should not drink and drive? Why does a woman have to be admitted to the intensive care unit to leave an abusive man? Experience is not the best teacher. God did not need the next generation to wander another forty years to teach them the lessons their parents didn't learn. The wisdom and failures of the previous generation could save them.

Wisdom Is a Giant Killer

King Solomon was a man of great wisdom. He wrote to the next generation:

- "Joyful is the person who finds wisdom, the one who gains understanding. For wisdom is more profitable than silver, and her wages are better than gold. Wisdom is more precious than rubies; nothing you desire can compare with her. She offers you long life in her right hand, and riches and honor in her left" (Proverbs 3:13-16 NLT).

- "And so, my children, listen to me, for all who follow my ways are joyful. Listen to my instruction and be wise. Don't ignore it. Joyful are those who listen to me, watching for me daily at my gates, waiting for me outside my home! For whoever finds me finds life and receives favor from the Lord. But those who miss me *injure themselves.* All who hate me **love death**" (Proverbs 8:32-36 NLT emphasis added).

Here, Solomon is trying to teach us how to love wisdom and how to avoid the experiments that failed him in life. Nothing compares to godly wisdom. The return of investment is incomparable to anything you possess.

Wisdom is the architect of dreams. It extends and blesses our lives. It releases peace and creativity. It gives sound judgment and discernment. It preserves safety. It increases our influence—our wealth and honor—to build what is in our heart. Wisdom was present in the beginning before the creation of oceans and before the boundaries and limits of the seas were set. Before the earth had form, the lights came on, and life was breathed into God's greatest creation humanity—*there was wisdom.* There was God. We need to ask God for wisdom as we make dreams and plans. Wisdom slays generational giants.

False Dreams

In 1978, the grisly images from Jonestown, Guyana, shocked the world. More than 900 people were dead because they missed God. They hated wisdom and believed a lie. When they arrived at Jonestown, it was not their dreamed utopia. It was a nightmare.

Their concerned relatives tried to save them and wrote an accusation against Jim Jones citing human rights violations such as:

- Prohibiting relatives from leaving Guyana by confiscating their passports and money.
- Stationing guards around Jonestown to prevent anyone from escaping.
- Prohibiting telephone calls.
- Prohibiting individual contacts with "outsiders."
- Censoring all incoming and outgoing mail.
- Extorting silence from relatives in the U.S. by threats to stop all communication.

One of the concerned relatives was Steven Katsaris, who wrote an affidavit in the accusation against Jim Jones after a failed attempt to bring his daughter home from Jonestown. In that affidavit, written on April 4, 1978, he stated, "I managed to tell my daughter that if she ever wanted to return home, a ticket would be waiting for her at the Embassy. When I told her of my belief in God and that somehow things would work out, she and another woman from the 'Church' were quick to point out to me that they do not believe in God."

Jones created a godless atmosphere of fear in Jonestown. He transferred his paranoia to his people. His members showed him their hearts, and he crushed them. He was a fraud. Imposter. Wolf in sheep's clothing. He tricked them into believing a false dream—into abandoning all godly wisdom—to their ultimate death. He assassinated Congressman Leo Ryan. He separated and killed family members right before their loved one's eyes. He told them because Ryan was dead, the government would storm Jonestown and take their children captive. Fear was the weapon he used to kill them. The people would have done anything to ensure they did not experience the same fate as Congressman Ryan and his crew.

In the ABC 20/20 special *Truth and Lies: Jonestown, Paradise Lost*, Jim Jones's biological son Stephen Jones spoke out against his father, yet referring to the "sickness" of the people—the victims of Jonestown—stated, "Jim Jones by himself can't kill 900 people." But society doesn't call a wife killed by her abusive husband "sick." We don't call an abducted woman or sex trafficking victims—kidnapped and held against their will—"sick." In the ABC documentary, survivors—including Stephen and Jim Jones Jr.—shared that Jones didn't like people leaving. He had a hard time with that.

Survivors, including Deborah Layton, sister of Larry Layton, who killed Congressman Ryan, also stated that Jones:

- had members sign false confessions early on
- had parents sign they were molesting children as a means of blackmail if they left

- had members sign blank pieces of paper to use against them if they left the Temple
- isolated people who wanted out of Jonestown— Jones kept them away from the main population, so they could not expose him
- offered defectors who tried to leave with Congressman Ryan $5,000 and their passports to stay
- ordered the congressman and defectors death then asked the members who stayed, "Is there any dissenting opinion?"
- had guards forcibly take children from the arms of their parents to kill them

Jones promised his followers heaven but created a living hell on earth. This is a sobering reminder that one wrong person, one wrong relationship, one sip, one five-second decision can cost you everything. On that fateful night, the people of Jonestown were screaming as Jones ordered their deaths. He had just killed those who defected at the Port Kaituma airstrip. Where could they run? The members had two choices: drink poison or be killed (by bullet, arrow, or injection). Stephen Jones, later in the ABC documentary, said this regarding the willingness of the members to follow his father: "You go along because you don't want the same thing to happen to you."

Jones killed 900 people with fear and false dreams. He weaponized poverty and racial disparity to brainwash his members with fear, hopelessness, and lies of a utopian commune. In a recorded interview Jones said, "I decided, how can I demonstrate my Marxism? The thought was, infiltrate the church." Jones used a fake pulpit to attract members and money and promote his brand of *apostolic socialism* where people had "all things in common." According to the *Washington Post*, before the massacre, the People's Temple had accumulated over seven million dollars in offshore bank accounts.

Jones deceived everyone. He fed and rehabilitated the homeless. Housed senior citizens. Fathered "fatherless" children. Provided free daycare. Showed personal concern for underserved populations. Filled unmet needs to gain their trust. Then, he slept with male and female members (many against their will). Preached profanity-laced messages. Stomped on the Bible. Cursed God. Abused and beat those who loved him. Eventually, he robbed, killed, and destroyed their dreams.

Don't confuse what happened in Jonestown with the church of Jesus Christ. Jim Jones did not belong to the church. The People's Temple was a cult, and Jones had the spirit of the Antichrist. (See 1 John 4:3).

Jesus is a life-giver. He heals. Redeems. Comforts. Loves. Forgives. Rescues and outlives generations. Jim Jones was a thief. A tyrant. A giant of his members' greatest fears. There was no God in his body. He brainwashed and betrayed his people—issuing death threats to them if they left him. Then, when Congressman Leo Ryan tried to take defectors back to the U.S. with him, Jones killed him in cold blood—at point blank range—ordering the others to die before government officials exposed what was really going on in Jonestown.

In 1 John 2:18-19, the apostle John wrote, "Dear children, the last hour is here. You have heard that the Antichrist is coming, *and already many such antichrists have appeared.* From this we know that the last hour has come. These people left our churches, but they never really belonged with us; otherwise, they would have stayed with us. When they left, it proved that they did not belong with us" (NLT, emphasis added).

Jim Jones *never* belonged to the church. He falsely advertised Jonestown—with infomercials, false promises, and forced testimonials—to trick members into liquidating all their property and investments to move there. But when they arrived at Jonestown, it was in the middle of a hot jungle with armed guards. It was a concentration camp with little food, and nothing he had promised. The people were starved and subjected to cruel labor. It was far from utopia. The experiment was fatal, proving that experience is not always the best teacher. *Wisdom is.* If God intended for us to learn everything by experience, he wouldn't have given us the Bible.

Jonestown was the *worst* teacher. It cost more than 900 people their lives, ripping people away from their families. But wisdom could have saved them. We can learn from the mistakes of others. Paul taught his spiritual son, Timothy, "Anyone who does not provide for relatives, and especially for immediate family members, has denied the faith and is worse than an unbeliever" (1 Timothy 5:8).

My cousin Omar once said, "Physical inheritance is transferred only once in a lifetime." That is true, but family history is made daily. Don't fall for relationships or mindsets that denigrate your family tree. Learn from the past. The people of Jonestown left an inheritance of pain, shame, suffering, ridicule, and defeat behind—yet a blueprint. A blueprint of how *not* to live. *Not* to isolate. *Not* to stay in abusive relationships or die. *Not* to give up your freedom of choice or speech—*ever*.

Lessons in the Wilderness

What can we learn from the Israelites?

The apostle Paul wrote this powerful reminder:

I don't want you to forget, dear brothers and sisters, about our ancestors in the wilderness long ago. *All* of them were guided by a cloud that moved ahead of them, and *all* of them walked through the sea on dry ground. In the cloud and in the sea, *all* of them were baptized as followers of Moses. *All* of them ate the same spiritual food, and *all* of them drank the same spiritual water. For they drank from the spiritual rock that traveled with them, and that rock was Christ. Yet God was not pleased with most of them, and their bodies were scattered in the wilderness. These things happened as a warning to us, so that we would not crave evil things as they did, or worship idols as some of them did. As the Scriptures say, "The people celebrated with feasting and drinking, and they indulged in pagan revelry." And we must not engage in sexual immorality as some of them did, causing 23,000 of them to die in one day. Nor should we put Christ to the test, as some of them did and then died from snakebites. And don't grumble as some of them did, and then were destroyed by the angel of death. *These things happened to them as examples for us.* They were written down to warn us who live at the end of the age. If you think you are standing strong, be careful not to fall. The temptations in your life are no different from what others experience. (1 Corinthians 10:1-13 NLT, emphasis added)

In the wilderness, a generation died, so a generation could live. A generation fell, so a generation could rise. What happened to Israel happens to us. We wander in one place because of giants. We refuse to confront our greatest fears. We let the fear of failure destroy our dreams. We grumble. We complain. We question leadership. We procrastinate. We sin. We crave free stuff. We feel overwhelmed when facing obstacles. We doubt God. The result? We die with unfulfilled dreams. The Israelites inspire us what to do and what not to do in life. They remind us that what God promises, he keeps stored up—waiting for us or our children to take. Because our lifetime is too small to contain everything promised to us. In the Old Testament, whenever God made a promise to someone, it *always* included their descendants.

Lessons in Haran

Have you ever set a goal, only to stop short—or give up—before you get there?

We find another generational lesson in Genesis 11:31-32, "One day Terah took his son Abram, his daughter-in-law Sarai (his son Abram's wife), and his grandson Lot (his son Haran's child) and moved away from Ur of the Chaldeans. He was headed for the land of Canaan, *but they stopped at Haran and settled there.* Terah lived for 205 years and died while still in Haran" (NLT, emphasis added).

Abraham's dad had a destination in mind—take his family to the land flowing with milk and honey. But somewhere along the line, he stopped. He stopped dreaming and settled. And when he settled, he died. So, God told Abram to leave his father's house: "Leave your native country, your relatives, and your father's family, and go to the land that I will show you. I will make you into a great nation. I will bless you and make you famous, and you will be a blessing to others. I will bless those who bless you and curse those who treat you with contempt. All the families on earth will be blessed through you" (Genesis 12:1-3 NLT).

God did not call you to settle. He calls us to move past the places our predecessors stopped. The lifestyle of mediocrity, passivity, and dissatisfaction was never to be our home. Who told you that was the best you could do? Every place you settle affects the next generation. Your children are watching every move you make—every dream you start and stop. Abraham, at 75, decided to leave his earthly inheritance for a vision God had given him. He was settled—with a wife and family affairs—but there was *more* God had for him. God wanted to make his name famous, distinguish him from predecessors who had settled, become stagnant, and died promise-less. He wanted to make him the father of something not seen yet. Abraham was going to be the father of faith. A pioneer of family history to bless generations to come. God was going to take this old man—with a dream—and make him a thousand times more than what he was, with just one seed.

God only needs one seed. Every seed He creates multiplies. He can take one book—one job, one business, one gift, one talent, one invention, one recipe, one album, one movie—and make your name famous. But you must leave the place of mourning. You must bury what has settled in your life and move forward. If you don't bury it, it will stink. If you don't bury your past, the stench of what you did will be unbearable. It will be a constant smell and reminder to you and people.

Today, are you settled, barren, comfortable, and in a familiar place? You don't have to stay there. You don't have to die in the same place—at the same age—your parents did. You can be different. You can go farther than they did. Even if your earthly parent doesn't want that for you, your Heavenly Father does.

The Lord told Abraham in Genesis: "Regarding Sarai, your wife—her name will no longer be Sarai. From now on her name will be Sarah. And I will bless her and give you a son from her! Yes, I will bless her richly, and she will become the mother of many nations. Kings of nations will be among her descendants" (17:15-16 NLT).

Without faith, Abraham and Sarah's dream of having a son—a royal family—would have died trapped inside of them. They would have settled being childless, with unfulfilled dreams—untapped potential crying to be birthed, but never receiving strength for it. So by faith—against all hope, with no child in sight—Abraham believed. *Will you?* The writer of Hebrews wrote: "And so from this one man, and he as good as dead, came descendants as numerous as the stars in the sky and as countless as the sand on the seashore" (Hebrews 11:12 NIV).

Who Will Succeed You?

Our church's late grandfather in the faith, Dr. Fred Roberts, once said, "You can't be a success, without a successor."

Whatever God promised you has the exponential power to make you multiply—to be numerous—to produce what you cannot see, dream, hope for, or imagine. Don't reduce your dream by human limitations, by the "Ishmaels" you created by human strength and will. A supernatural seed of promise—the birth of what seems impossible—is coming no matter how long it takes. What you fail to possess, He will give to your children and the next generation that succeeds you.

God promised Abraham that leaders, rulers, and presidents would come from his and Sarah's family tree. God made this promise when they had no children or hope for a family—let alone future generations. In Genesis 15:5, He took Abram outside and said to him, "Look up into the sky and count the stars if you can. That's how many descendants you will have!" (NLT).

God gave Abraham a vision of success by showing him His limitless creation. He created us to be in His image— to be success*ful*. Filled with success. Filled with favor. King Solomon wrote: "He holds *success* in store for the upright, he is a shield to those whose walk is blameless, for he guards the course of the just and protects the way of his faithful ones" (Proverbs 2:7-8 NIV, emphasis added).

God holds *success*—and all that He has promised— in store for the upright. That means success is waiting. It comes by the decisions we make. Even when I'm not ready for it, God holds it in *store* for me. He takes wisdom stored in one season, to open up His storehouses in another. I may not see it yet, but when I least expect it—when nothing is left, and everything has dried up—God releases what He has kept in store for me. Likewise, He makes and keeps ready what He promised you. He waited for Noah to finish building the ark before He sent rain. God kept Jericho walled up for the Israelites. He didn't allow the giants to storm out of the walled city and defeat them in the wilderness. Their fame—the terror of who they were— had already melted the Canaanite hearts with fear. (See Joshua 2:10-11 NIV).

Every year the land was held in the hands of giants, its property—wealth, precious metals, surplus, prosperity, and resources—appreciated for God's people. Even when they spent 430 years in Egyptian slavery, it was waiting for them. When the people took a forty-year detour because of sin, it was waiting for them. After seventy years in exile, God still preserved the land for His people to return and restore it—to give them hope and a future.

What God stores up for you, He pays up. His gifts and callings are without repentance. In other words, God hasn't rescinded His call upon your life because of what you have done. The biggest lie of the enemy is that we cannot overcome our past sins and become what we thought we should be by now. But God doesn't make a mistake. He's no man's debtor. Every year you don't take possession of what God promised you, it increases in value. It grows. The giants you don't kill in your lifetime live—sometimes to the third and fourth generation. If you won't kill them, He keeps them breathing for your children and grandchildren—biological or spiritual—to confront and defeat one day.

Satan would love to convince us that time has tolled. That it's too late to restore the things we lost. To repair our broken relationships. To make redemptive decisions. To change our lifestyle. He wants to convince us the only option is to return to what we used to be. But we have the power to curse every contaminated and critical spirit in our lives.

A Parent's Influence

We transmit the behaviors we don't change—the traumas we don't heal.

A parent's influence on their children is powerful—even later as adults.

My mom was a hard worker. As a single mother, she did whatever it took to maintain the house we lived in after her divorce from my stepdad. As a result, after traveling as an evangelist for years, she started a church in Los Angeles, California, in or around 1985. I had to remain back in San Francisco to finish high school, but my mom was resilient. She kept the mortgage paid, the refrigerator filled, and supplied all my physical needs. But I was alone. I practically raised myself through high school. My emotional love tank grew empty. I spent weeks at a time unsupervised—*all alone.*

Then, out of rebellion, I began to cut class with a group of friends. I stole my mom's car keys and drove her car around San Francisco without a license. I wanted to be popular. By senior year, I missed so many classes and assignments in my English class, my teacher said I wouldn't graduate. My mom rushed home to schedule a parent-teacher conference with him. At her insistence, he agreed to let me graduate only if I didn't miss a class, miss an assignment, wasn't tardy or late, and scored a "B" or above in all tests and quizzes. I appreciated my mom doing that for me. It wasn't easy, but I did it—I graduated. During that season, God showed me if I put my mind to anything, I could accomplish it.

After graduation, I was excited to move to Los Angeles to join my mother and live with her after achieving this great feat. I wanted to make her proud of me. When I arrived in Los Angeles, the church was doing very well. Over a thousand people weekly were being touched by the presence of God. But my mom didn't have a place large enough for me to live with her. She lived in a studio apartment, so I had to stay with one of the members in the church. I was heartbroken. I wanted to be with my mom, not a stranger. No one could take her place. But I suppressed the disappointment for years, trying to move on and be a "man."

Eventually, I was married and started a new family and business. My wife and I bought a house and raised three kids together. I coached my two sons' basketball teams to three consecutive championships. Became a sports journalist. A pastor. A radio host. A healthcare advocate and motivational speaker. I influenced hundreds of thousands of people, yet deep down I was still hurting from childhood events from my past. Initially, I told everybody I was fine. But as years passed, I realized I wasn't. The voids in our childhood never fill themselves.

Eventually, I was able to admit to my wife, "I wish my mom had a place for me when I graduated." It still hurt after all those years. My mother did the best she could. She is a great mom and Nana—lavishing our kids with cash or gifts for birthdays and Christmases. She and my mother-in-law, Vijaya, are very generous to them. But in my own early childhood, I noticed when my mom left me out or didn't get me a gift for Christmas, it bothered me. I don't know why. There is nothing she could give me I could not buy myself. I guess it reminded me of all the holidays we missed together when she was away traveling to support us. I am very grateful for everything my mom provided for me growing up. When I was eighteen, she helped me purchase my first car, but I wanted so much more. I wanted her. But her work, as a single parent, didn't permit that.

Raising Adult Children

We underestimate the impact our parenting decisions have on our kids later—after they become adults. As a parent, we don't come with a manual to raise children. We are learning on the go. As fathers, sometimes we are hard on our sons, because we want to create a better model of a man than what we are. We just can't imagine bringing in another generation of males that look like us, fall like us, or get angry like us. We want our kids to get something right that we didn't. But we tend to mess that up too. In school or college, we train for everything we do in life or occupation—except parenting.

When my oldest son, Joshua, was a teenager, I was very hard on him. I remember one day grabbing his shirt collar and pushing him against a wall while my wife and younger son grabbed me away from him. It was a very traumatic incident. We were all crying. Later, I took my oldest son in my arms to cradle his 6 foot1 inch frame while weeping and repeatedly saying, "Dad is so sorry for doing that. I lost my temper. That will never happen again." Later in his 20's, I snapped at him for not doing something I asked, and while scolding him, I sensed him shutting down. My harmful anger imprint from the past was a giant. I immediately shifted gears and told him, "Son, I love you and always want the best for you. This is just a suggestion."

In 2 Corinthians 1:4, the apostle Paul wrote: "He comforts us in all our troubles so that we can comfort others. When they are troubled, we will be able to give them the same comfort God has given us" (NLT).

But it's hard to give what we haven't received ourselves personally.

I tried to give my children everything I had and didn't have growing up. This created conflicts. When they were hurt, I was a great encourager, but not always a great comforter. I didn't have many experiences of being comforted myself growing up. While my mom traveled for ministry, I raised myself. When she was home, she moved me with words. Therefore, when I was sick, lonely, or discouraged, I used my words to get out of the bed and push through it. When people didn't believe in me, I had to encourage myself with words to show up to school the next day—often, stuffing and ignoring the pain or rejection I struggled with. That was my normal. So, I pushed my kids the same way. When they received bad news, I showed them how to pray for themselves and speak over their dreams. But they needed more. They needed my presence, validation, and empathy too. Rarely, did I respond to their tears and disappointment by holding them in my arms, and saying, "I'm so sorry you are hurting. What I can do to take the pain away?"

When Jesus ascended, He told the disciples, "I will ask the Father to give you another Helper [Comforter, et al] to be with you forever" (John 14:16 AMP).

We must be tangibly present in the lives of people.

As a parent of adult children, I want to be so keen to the things I didn't give my children enough of growing up. To be sensitive to those triggers I can push that remind them of the past. I want to show them my heart, even when they don't show me theirs.

Malachi 4:6 declares that in the last days, "He will turn the hearts of the fathers to their children, and the hearts of the children to their fathers *[a reconciliation produced by repentance]*, so that I will not come and strike the land with a curse [of complete destruction]" (AMP, italics added).

God requires me to turn my heart to my children before they turn their hearts to me. When we turn our hearts to them, we permit them to turn to us—to heal wounds of the past. Before the next generation turns, we must turn. We must produce reconciliation by powerful repentance. We must admit where we have failed. We must be the example and take the high road. Sometimes when you call your teenage or adult children, or take a step forward to stay a part of their lives—they run from you. But don't stop calling them. Don't stop reaching. Don't shut off emotionally. Don't leave them. You're the older adult. Love them. Silence from an adult child may actually be a cry that they need something you are not giving them. Your adult children will come around when they see you come around.

They will mature as you mature. And when they do, a relationship needs to be present to bridge the gap.

Recently, my mom apologized for leaving me in San Francisco during my high school years. In one conversation, she changed the landscape and health of our family tree. Her apology did not change the past, but eased the pain associated with it. It altered history.

As mentioned in earlier chapters, my father was not present in my life growing up. The only memory I have of him as a child is the infamous "coke" incident. When I was forty-nine, I asked my mom why he wasn't around more. She proceeded to tell me the painful story of my father taking her to the hospital the day I was born, then leaving her alone, *at the age of 18*, to give birth to me while he went to preach at church. I was heartbroken. So many questions swirled around my mind: "Why wouldn't he stand by her side?" "Why didn't he want to see the birth of his first son?" She then shared that, after I was born, he would make promises to come pick me up and then he would break them. I would jump up and down in excitement to see him, and when he didn't show, I'd break down crying. While she was speaking, tears welled up in my eyes as I began to feel those painful emotions re-emerge and grip my heart. As a forty-nine-year-old man, I felt five again—as if it had just happened yesterday. I suppressed all the pain, all those years, but the hole was still there.

As giant killers, we must fill the gaps, left by our parents, in our parenting style. Parenting is not necessarily punishment, but presence. When our children marry and raise a family, they must do the same—fill in the holes we leave in our parenting. My wife asked me recently, "Was your dad there for any of his other kids?" I shared with her, based on my brief experience with him as an adult and my only recollection of him as a child, probably not. She replied: "If so, how amazing it is to see a complete reversal of the generation pattern set by him. You went from having no dad around, to being *all in* for your kids. Being at every game. Every recital. Every play and musical. Every graduation. Being a witness to see them get accepted into college, paying their tuition, and watching them pursue their dreams and degrees. Being an influence on how they should raise the bar and their kids."

That's when God shared this thought with me: "One person—one giant killer can transform the next generation. At any time in our lives, we are the Joshua generation. The generation that must face the giants of our predecessors to rewrite our family history. You are never too old to have a giant. You are never too old to have a daddy or momma issue. We either run from Goliath or run at him."

In this season of raising giant killers, I am learning not to underestimate the impact I have on my now adult kids. It is not merely enough for me to say to them, "I should have been a better dad." I have to identify pockets of unresolved hurt, anger, or embarrassment I may have caused and say, "Son, daughter, I was thinking about when you were twelve, how I made you [name the incident] and how embarrassed that must've made you. I was wrong to do that. That was anger and pride. It should have never happened. Will you please forgive me for that?"

I don't want to be a giant to them—triggering past hurts with current behavior. As parents, we raise the adults we see later. But that doesn't change their personal responsibility for choices in life. You can be the perfect father or mother and your children will still fail you. But don't become critical. Don't tell them "I told you so" when they fail. Give them a different model of parenthood than you received from your parents.

Turn your hearts to them.

The future generations belong to us. We get to change any unhealthy imprints left by our parents and predecessors, by how we love, speak up, forgive, raise, and influence our children's children. What my dad failed to do in his generation may not all be undone by mine. But if I begin the healing, God can finish it.

My daughter, Jasmine, is a great example of creating new family history. She is exceptional in moving your heart with unique gifts that take your breath away. While I grew up learning how to give expensive gifts to people, Jasmine gave the best gifts. Gifts of time. Memories. Photos. One Father's Day, when she was an adolescent, she had a tie created with her and her two brother's picture on it. For my wife's 50th birthday, she printed out 50 pictures, gathered her brothers, and hung 50 balloons in the ceiling with pictures spanning her mom's life.

Jasmine refuses to be forgotten.

As an adult, she has continued the trait of inspiring us to do more than just buy material things. She hates just sitting in a movie theater where there is no quality family time spent. Even when she doesn't say it, she inscribes what is in her heart on yours. She loves doing small things that have huge impacts for years to come.

You can too.

As giant killers, we determine how people remember us.

CHAPTER 13

THE WILDERNESS

When God gives us a dream—calls us for a specific purpose, it cannot be revoked. However, we can abandon it in a place called "the wilderness." Israel's wilderness was a land of forgetfulness and separation—a place not designed to be inhabited. Nothing grew there. It was a dry and infertile land.

When I started my first business, I was only nineteen years old. In 1989, I was working for a collection law firm when a few of us left for other jobs. A co-worker of mine found an attorney who worked in trusts and wills and proposed starting a collection law division. He asked me to join him there as the Director of Recovery while he worked in Business Development. One summer, he took a trip to Hawaii with his fiancée and took money out of the bank account without the knowledge of the attorney. She was furious. She separated from him and wanted to close the division. I was able to persuade her to keep it running under my leadership. A year later, I negotiated a separation to start a corporation that would pay her a retainer to supervise letter writing and potentially litigate cases. I moved the company to Torrance, California, and in those years made a lot of money at a very young age. But I wasn't ready for it. No one had ever taught me how to be responsible with that kind of revenue. I eventually stopped paying clients and ended up losing my Torrance office. I tried to open an office in Orange County, but it closed too. Nothing was working. I was fighting the will of God, who wanted me to lose everything in order to gain him.

That was my wilderness. A season of loss disguised as a season of discovery. What I lost in that business, God restored and multiplied in my current one. Not just money, but Him. I heard someone once say, "Sometimes, you don't realize all you need is God, until all you have is God."

Moses spent two stints of forty years each in the wilderness. His first season in the wilderness was to prepare him for his calling. It was where God spoke to him from the burning bush (Exodus 3). When God called him, Moses felt unqualified. He doubted his speaking ability and influence to face a giant like Pharaoh. As a stutterer with no previous experience, he responded to the call of God saying, "Lord, please send someone else."

God replied to Moses's excuse of not being a good speaker in Exodus 4:10-12, "…Who gave human beings their mouths? Who makes them deaf or mute? Who gives them sight or makes them blind? Is it not I, the LORD? Now go; I will help you speak and will teach you what to say" (NIV).

God asks the same to us today: "Who gave you that dream or vision? Who gave you that voice? Who gave you the gift to write, create, animate, build, lead, preach, practice medicine, law, or whatever? Your Egypt, Pharaoh, or opposition is nothing compared to me. The system that has enslaved your mind in doubt is about to be broken."

God doesn't let us out of our call that easily—no matter what our handicap, physical limitation, or circumstance. No matter what He has called us to do—who He called you to be—this call will not be revoked. He will allow forty years in the wilderness—on the backside of a desert, where no one sees you, no one knows what is inside of you—to prepare you to stand before giants.

The Three Stages of the Wilderness

The wilderness is a season where we are isolated from our dream—what God promised us. The Israelites went through three stages of testing we must also go through in life.

1. Reaffirmation

In Exodus 7, God reaffirmed an unsure and unqualified Moses by telling him, "I have made you like God to Pharaoh." He didn't say, "I am 'making' you," but "You already are like God to him. You have my authority now. You will stand in my place in front of Pharaoh. Whatever you command, say, and decree, I will do."

God has made you like God to your giant. He has put His spirit in you to kill every one of your giants for the next generation.

Exodus 7:7 says: "Moses and Aaron did just as the Lord commanded them. Moses was eighty years old and Aaron eighty-three when they spoke to Pharaoh" (NIV). The rule of Pharaoh that lived in Moses's forties, still lived in his eighties, because giants don't grow old and die. They grow bigger.

But it's never too late to speak to your giant (or what has enslaved you). We are never too old to start obeying God. Yet we all need reaffirmation that we are still called—that we can still be used. That despite our mistakes and inadequacies, we are still God's ambassadors—His arms, His feet, and voice. The apostle Paul declared that the gifts and calling of God on our life are irrevocable. He never withdraws them once they are given. He does not change His mind about you and I ever—even if we wasted forty years of our life running from Him (Romans 11:29).

2. Identification

God said: "Your brother Aaron will be your prophet." God was identifying Aaron to Moses as compensation in an area where he was weak. He was telling Moses, "You don't get to make excuses for not doing what you were called to do. No matter how hard Pharaoh's heart is—no matter what he does to you, you don't get a pass. Keep showing up every morning as if you never failed. Keep speaking through your brother Aaron."

Our vision or call will make us question our anointing unless we identify people who can cover our weaknesses and make us better. God sends human compensation to help us become profitable or successful in an enterprise or ministry. When people around us—in the same place of their ability, skills, creativity, and accomplishments— are not being successful from year to year, making old mistakes not new mistakes, forcing us to engage in corrective action at the expense of engaging with our most productive people, and requiring us to re-teach them the basics of the job function, we need to reevaluate if they are the ones God has called to our team.

The wrong people—or lack of the right ones—can be the greatest hindrance and distraction to any God-given vision. We must surround ourselves with people who are not only complimentary, but better than us, in the areas where we are weak or insufficient. If in our weakness, we can do better than others can in their strength, we should redefine their role and purpose on our team.

3. Multiplication

God was preparing to multiply His signs and wonders in Egypt. God told Moses:

> But I know that the king of Egypt will not let you go unless a mighty hand forces him. So I will raise my hand and strike the Egyptians, performing all kinds of miracles among them. Then at last he will let you go. And I will cause the Egyptians to look favorably on you. They will give you gifts when you go so you will not leave empty-handed. Every Israelite woman will ask for articles of silver and

gold and fine clothing from her Egyptian neighbors and from the foreign women in their houses.
You will dress your sons and daughters with these,
stripping the Egyptians of their wealth. (Exodus
3:19-22 NLT)

Through the hardening of Pharaoh's heart, God set up
His people to obtain—from the Egyptians—whatever they
needed. Whether silver, gold, clothes, or shoes, nothing
they asked for was denied by the Egyptians. By then,
Moses had gained quite a reputation in Egypt. His name
and exploits had spread across the land—there was no
one like him (Deuteronomy 34:10-12).

Since the beginning of time, God has always used
leaders and giant killers to rescue generations. In the
book of Judges, they are called "deliverers." Today, He
still delivers families, neighborhoods, and nations into our
hands. Not for our namesake, *but His*. He brought Israel
out of Egypt, out of the wilderness—into the Promised
Land—for His name's sake. He kept His promise in spite
of their rebellion, so nations would see He is faithful—
even when His people are not.

In Egypt, God was taking the Israelites from the best
land, once given to them (Genesis 45:10), to a territory
they had to take by force. God was determined to give
them something greater. It was a land they could appre-
ciate because up to this point, they had never fought for
anything in their life. They were used to things being given
to them—even the straw to make bricks in Egypt.

We can't live the rest of our lives waiting for someone to give us something. Moses had to appear ten times before Pharaoh and release ten plagues to change his hardened heart. Moses kept doing what God told him to do, but God kept hardening Pharaoh's heart. Even after their release, Pharaoh came charging after them in the Red Sea. Moses was doing the right thing. But he yielded no results until he repeatedly demonstrated he was committed to the call of God on his life.

How many times will you show up? Apply to schools? Apply for the promotion? Write the appeal? Pray for the miracle?

Never get weary doing "the right thing." Do what you can control. Multiply where you were supposed to lose. That word "multiply" in Hebrew is "rabab" and means "to be or become many; to abound, become numerous, great, increase, or more in number."

God still multiplies us in hostile environments.

Love Where You Are

We must love the place we are as if it were our destiny. We enter into new seasons by embracing bad ones. This is the process and the preparation for greatness. We cannot become impatient or depressed because of hostile people. When you are doing what you love, they won't matter. You will endure whatever obstacles that come and face any challenges that arise. The obstacles we face today in our "wilderness" push us from comfort into multiplication. In the wilderness, God stretches us to do things we don't want to do, can't do, or aren't good at. To do things seemingly with no significance to our dream or degree. To work on jobs that fail to highlight our natural gift or ability.

Why? Because God needs to deal with every weakness—every critical voice—in us. Every "I can't." Every giant of pride. This is the place where God manifests Himself, where He will compensate us with people that help build, lead, and accomplish what is in our heart (Isaiah 43:4). This is a scary place: where the enemies we see today, we will see no more; where giants from our past drown. In the wilderness, God is preparing to bless us unexpectedly, so we will not leave one season the same way we entered.

The wilderness was not a death sentence. It was a preparation for the land of the Israelites' wildest dreams. But in the Book of Numbers, we read:

> Then the whole community began weeping aloud, and they cried all night. Their voices rose in a great chorus of protest against Moses and Aaron. 'If only we had died in Egypt, or even here in the wilderness!' they complained. *"Why is the Lord taking us to this country only to have us die in battle?* Our wives and our little ones will be carried off as plunder! Wouldn't it be better for us to return to Egypt?" Then they plotted among themselves, "Let's choose a new leader and go back to Egypt." (Numbers 14:1-4 NLT)

The Israelites wanted to stay on welfare, rather than fight for what God had promised them. So, they protested. Grumbled. Murmured. Questioned leadership. Have you ever been there? Ever complain about some dissatisfaction in life? Your pay? Position? Parents? Professors? Bosses? Church leaders? Hard work? Living conditions? A spouse or in-law? An inheritance or lack thereof?

That word *murmur* means "to make complaining remarks or noises under one's breath; it is a complaint half-suppressed or uttered in a low, muttering voice (the movement of the lips without the production of articulate speech)."

In medical terms, a *murmur* is an abnormal sound—usually emanating from the heart—that indicates a diseased condition. The Israelites were diagnosed with a heart condition called discontentment. They were serial murmurers. Here, they said, "Let's go back to the place the Lord delivered us from. Let's not finish what we started. Let's quit. It's been great, but giants are ahead." The Israelites wanted to return to a life that was no longer there. Every trace of their past life had drowned in the Red Sea—yet they still craved it.

It was here the people began to prefer Pharaoh over God. They began to crave what humanity can provide—man's provision instead of God's promise. Don't let hardships blind you from what God is doing. Don't think you can do less, because giants (or people) say you can't do more. Do what men say you cannot do. Giants make kings. Goliath was an obstacle God used to make David a king and champion. Today, He still does exceedingly, super-abundantly, far above all we dare ask, think, dream, hope, pray for, or imagine (Ephesians. 3:20 AMP).

All Things Work Together for Good

God calls Abraham when he is a heathen man, uncertain of his destiny. He is promised a son—to be a great nation. But he wasn't. Romans 4:19 says his body and wife's womb were as good as dead. Sometimes God has to go to the grave to summon new life. He has to crucify or put to death what is no longer working. Abraham did not see the promise of his own son Isaac until he was one hundred years old.

Likewise, every dream—in harmony with your destiny—has an appointed time. What delays it? *Immaturity.* We do not have what we dream—we have not reached our goal—because of impatience. Things seem dead. Too often, we quit in the "process." We don't fall in love with it. We stop being great in "little" things.

In the book, *A Tale of Three Kings: A Study in Brokenness*, author Gene Edwards writes, "Beginning empty-handed and alone frightens the best of men. It also speaks volumes of just how sure they are that God is with them."

Jesus is worth more than we lost.

In the wilderness, God builds consistency. He determines what we can be trusted with. If we are ready for more, He proves us. He trains our hands to kill giants. He helps us get over what was lost and build on what is left.

He enables us to take possession of our highest dreams. He watches to see if we are faithful—relentless in sowing when nothing is growing.

Don't resist the chastening of the Lord in the wilderness seasons of your life. Embrace it. When God goes before us, He sees things before we do. Sometimes He hardens the hearts of people to build consistency in the pursuit of our dreams. One day before Pharaoh—one thing done, one application, one job interview, one apology, one day sober, one counseling session, one day working hard, one client signed, one word spoken by faith—won't do it. We must build consistency.

Scary Dreams

Your dream must be a giant or step that scares you. It must push you into unfamiliar territory to meet opportunity. It must develop and prepare you now for what lies ahead. My year of being on welfare inspired me for the years of making millions.

While speaking in South Africa, I heard a billionaire say, *"The perspective I needed to make my first million, was not the perspective I needed to make my first billion."* God wants to show you the width, height, and length of His love and plan for you. But everything in life changes with or by perspective. Our perspective—point of reference in life—has great power. The apostle Paul wrote to the church in Corinth:

No eye has seen, no ear has heard, and no mind has imagined what God has prepared for those who love him. But it was to us that God revealed these things by his Spirit. For his Spirit searches out everything and shows us God's deep secrets. No one can know a person's thoughts except that person's own spirit, and no one can know God's thoughts except God's own Spirit. And we have received God's Spirit (not the world's spirit), so we can know the wonderful things God has freely given us. (1 Corinthians 2:9-12 NLT)

We need perspective. That word *perspective* is an interesting word. It was influenced by the Italian word *prospettiva*, an artists' term and figuratively meaning, a "mental outlook over time." *Perspective* is the "art of drawing objects so as to give the appearance of distance or depth." We need to understand why things are coming at us—why things are in the scene dormant, but not yet reality. We need to understand what appears in the scene—yet in recession—about to leap into our lives. We need to see things present to the eye, but not yet called into existence.

Too often, we see something in the scene or background of our life, but don't know how far it is from us. That's where perspective comes in. Perspective will help you make sense of what you are going through—where you are—and start turning fear into doors. But if the only perspective we have is ours, we won't see very far.

God's Perfect Will

Before I was married, I struggled with perspective. I often wondered what God's "perfect" will was versus His "permissive" will. Questions flooded my mind like: What should I study in college? Who should I marry? When should I build a church, business, or training center? But in that pursuit, I lost focus. I became distracted. In time, I learned that choosing God's perfect or permissive will, and living with that decision, is irrelevant to who you become.

God is not concerned about what we are accumulating, but who we are becoming in the fierce pursuit of our dream. His focus is on what we *will* be, not *who* we are. Joseph's path through prison wasn't ideal. The apostle Paul struggled through closed doors, beatings, and imprisonment. Moses spent two forty-year stints in the wilderness and never entered the Promised Land.

As we become who God is making us, we don't cower in shame and hiding. We celebrate wins. We learn from losses. We become great decision-makers—great responders in life. It doesn't matter what we haven't accomplished yet— how many doors have closed, who we didn't marry, what relationship or business idea failed. The question is, who did we become? How have we grown in each moment? What have we done with each loss? Did we get better? Did we gain a new, fresh perspective—a greater dependence upon God?

Sometimes we let what we haven't accomplished, diminish who we are becoming. We let it affect our perspective. We don't allow God to finish the beautiful masterpiece He is making from the ashes of our lives. In the wilderness, you realize, you are exactly where God wants you to be.

Five Lessons in the Wilderness

We must pass through the wilderness to achieve what God has promised. Giants stand in the way of your highest dream (1 Peter 2:21). They are coming. But in periods of preparation, power comes. God gives us skill in times of waiting. Times of separation. Times of confusion. Jesus spent forty days in the wilderness before ministry. The disciples spent three years with Jesus before he released them. If you are in a period of preparation, don't be discouraged. God does great things in prepared vessels. He works in men and women through the work of the Holy Spirit. He speaks to us in new places, new seasons, and new ways. He used an insignificant burning bush to speak to Moses in the wilderness. When Moses was commanded to take off his sandals in Exodus 3:5, God was saying, "Get used to the wilderness. This is your home for a season. Take off anything that separates you from Me."

We see five lessons the Israelites learned in the wilderness.

1. We cannot possess fame in Jericho, without making a name for ourselves in the wilderness.

In Deuteronomy 2:24-25, God told a discouraged Israelite family, "Now get moving! Cross the Arnon Gorge. Look, I will hand over to you Sihon the Amorite, king of

Heshbon, and I will give you his land. Attack him and begin to occupy the land. Beginning today I will make people throughout the earth terrified because of you. When they hear reports about you, they will tremble with dread and fear" (NLT).

In the forty years of wilderness, God was determined to show His children how to conquer smaller cities before He would give them bigger ones. Before they got another shot at Jericho, they had to overcome what was in front of them. How can you conquer the dream in your heart, if you still can't conquer cleaning your house? A bad temper? Watching pornography? Paying your creditors?

In that season where it seems there is no growth, what victories are you accumulating? What are you overcoming? Job 17:9 says, "The righteous keep moving forward, and those with clean hands become stronger and stronger."

While you are awaiting another crack at Jericho, are you getting better? Are you still confronting giants in your life? Still writing? Acting? Drawing? Putting bids in? Worshiping? Giving? Praying for people? Are you thriving in the place where people hate you? Despite the places you have failed Him and the wasted opportunities, God still wants to use you.

Stubborn hearts are often a sign we have won—that God has given us the head of our giant (Deuteronomy 2:30-36). God gave the Israelites every hard heart. Every last city. No walls were too strong for them. No single opposition proved too much for them. God will give you that boss or client who has hardened their heart towards you. He will give you the contract you thought was too big for you.

2. In the wilderness, we live by every word that proceeds *"daily"* out of the mouth of God.

In Deuteronomy 3:3-11, King Og was thirteen feet six inches tall, and yet God handed him and all his people over to the children of Israel. Not a single person survived. Before they took Jericho, God gave His children a taste of what it felt like to take a city. Likewise, He will provide us with a taste of what it feels like—to hit a game-winning shot, score a winning touchdown, hit a walk-off home run, get a promotion, defeat a lion or bear—before we kill a Goliath.

When I started my second business in 2000, we were struggling badly. I remember logging into my bank and seeing an extra $10,000 in the account. I called the bank and told them, "There is an error in my account. An extra $10,000 I did not deposit is showing. Can you reverse this?" The customer service rep, said, "I don't see an error. I cannot reverse the deposit—this is your money." I told the representative, "Lady, this is not my money and I am broke. Remove the money from the account before I spend it." She repeated the same thing, and I hung up. I continued to call the next four days. Every representative told me the same thing. Finally, on the fifth day, the bank discovered their error and reversed the money. As I stared at my bank account—almost in the negative—the Lord spoke a word to me, "Son, that deposit was just a sign of the type of deposits I am preparing to entrust you with."

God is constantly preparing us in the present, for what He has put in our future. Everything—no matter how much we hate it—has compensation. Every season has a purpose. We cannot afford to be critical—to miss what God is trying to teach us in this season. The older generation of the Israelites took sixty smaller walled cities before their children ever marched against Jericho. Remember the lessons God is teaching you. Remember to use your platform to bring honor and glory to Him. If we do, He will give us the wealth of our oppressors, positions we are not qualified for, houses we have not built, vineyards we have not planted—all for His glory.

But don't *desire* wealth. Desire God. If we never get rich—if we never get the dream house, car, or position we want—God wants to know *if He is enough for us.* If He is all we need. If we will live by His word *alone.* Whenever we seek wealth and appetites first, we create idols. We put created things—instead of God—on the throne of our lives. But God said, "Seek me first." Die to every form of *desire* vying to be first place in your life. Because when your perspectives are right, your heart will be right. And when your heart is right, treasure is found.

3.   Plateaus are signals of something bigger ahead.

At a certain point, the Israelites hit a plateau—a ceiling (Deuteronomy 3:10). It seemed like their prayers couldn't get them any farther in the wilderness. Have you reached a plateau in your life, relationships, career, or ministry? A place of dissatisfaction with nowhere else to go? If so, God is offering you an invitation to cross the place your predecessors stopped at—to cross Jordan. To leave your old life and enter new territory. New territory in your faith. Your ministry. Your marriage. Your gift, skill, and expertise. To face bigger competition and giants.

You've written newsletters, but now God wants to use you to write books. You've worked in your own kitchen—cooked for everyone else and their grandma—but now God wants to give you a catering business or restaurant. You've written screenplays in college, but now He wants to catapult your production onto Broadway, film, or television. You've worked at the position for ten years, but now God wants to give you the company. You've generated millions, but now God wants to do more than make money through you—He wants to make disciples.

When we fill a cup, we stop. We create a limit of how much we can have—forcing ourselves to come back for more. But in the wilderness, God brings us into a season of overflow. Where instead of stopping at one vessel, we borrow more. We pour the oil of our anointing and creativity—our gift—into the lives of many, meeting every need.

What is that plateau in your life? Where have you reached a ceiling and leveled off? It's time to blow the lid off your expectations.

4. We cannot leave where we are until we pack our bags.

Have you ever noticed that we pack differently, depending on where we are going?

If we are going somewhere temporarily, like on vacation, we pack seasonally—only what we need for the trip. We don't carry excess baggage. But if we are going somewhere permanently—like moving to a different residence or city—while packing, we throw away junk we don't use anymore. In Joshua 1:10-11, the children of Israel were ordered to pack their bags. Throw out stuff they didn't need. Bring only what's necessary. Pack light. Get rid of everything accumulated that had been keeping them down.

It is popular opinion that African American people should not be in horror movies. Because if we star in any non-comedy scary flick, we are going to die first. Why? It would not be believable if we survived to the end. It's not that we don't have the instinct to stay alive, *it's because we wouldn't be there.* We wouldn't go into the dark, creepy attic with voices. We wouldn't play the scary videotape where everyone dies after watching it. We wouldn't see our daughter sucked into the television set in the living room and go upstairs to sleep. We wouldn't live on Elm Street. We wouldn't camp at Camp Crystal Lake. We hate camping. And if we did go camping, we would question a guy in a hockey mask and gear—near a hot humid lake in the summer. If you remember in the 1979 horror flick *Amityville Horror*, George Lutz at one point is screaming at the haunted spirits in his house, "What do you want from

us? This is my house!" If that was a black man, and the
spirit said, "Get out," we are out. We are packing our bags
and leaving.

So God—the Spirit of Light—said through Joshua, "Get
out—pack your bags. This place is haunted and cursed
with bad decisions. It is a graveyard of disobedience. It
is not your permanent residence. Leave now. Anyone who
stays here for a prolonged time dies. This ground is soiled
by the blood of old, grumbling, complaining, and critical
people who contaminated your dreams. People who didn't
work together, who didn't trust Me in the worst of circumstances. So, pack your bags. This is your three-day eviction
notice. I'm kicking you out. I'm letting them fire you. I'm
allowing the contract to be lost so that I can take you into
something better. I'm cutting off welfare, so you can eat
what I promised" (Joshua 1:11-15-author's paraphrase).

The day the Israelites ate the produce of the land, the
manna in the wilderness stopped (Joshua 5:12). Because
a new home was waiting for their footsteps on the other
side. Every tribe had to work together. Every tribe was
required to help each other possess their territory. Nothing
was gained in isolation. No one could say, "I have done
this in my own strength." No one could glory in their own
flesh. (See Joshua 1:13-15).

Do you want to be a giant killer in your generation?
Do you want to manage million- or billion-dollar decisions
for yourself or others? Before we can possess a dream,
we must help someone else possess theirs. The Israelites
needed God and each other. We need people. If you don't

have a vision yet, get behind someone who has one, and God will give you your own. Pack your bags. Get your house in order. Evict your giants. Jericho is just ahead.

5. Giants are in our future.

God did not tell the Israelites the seven enemies keeping them from their destiny were giants. He doesn't always reveal obstacles when He reveals dreams. But He arms us with words that are weapons. In Deuteronomy 7:17-20, Moses told the Israelites:

> Perhaps you will think to yourselves, "How can we ever conquer these nations that are so much more powerful than we are?" But don't be afraid of them! Just remember what the Lord your God did to Pharaoh and to all the land of Egypt. Remember the great terrors the Lord your God sent against them. You saw it all with your own eyes! And remember the miraculous signs and wonders, and the strong hand and powerful arm with which he brought you out of Egypt. The Lord your God will use this same power against all the people you fear. And then the Lord your God will send terror to drive out the few survivors still hiding from you! (NLT)

What is the name of the giant speaking in your life today? Is it cancer or sickness? Fear? Dissatisfaction? Pride? Addictions? Laziness? Procrastination? Sin?

Uncertainty of where you are going to live or work next month? What is its name? How will you beat it?

God has promised to put the fear of us in any giant seen or hiding. But don't think He will require anything less from us than He expected from previous generations. We must live and not die in the wilderness. The next generation needs us to survive to tell our story. We must cross over to take our city—little by little, step by step—until the things that kept us from getting there are erased.

No excuses are allowed. Excuses harden our heart. They hinder change. Steal our dreams. Feed procrastination. When God moved the Israelites from the wilderness to the Promised Land, they could not do things the way their parents had. They had to disinherit their fears to face the giants they were afraid of. They had to break out of familiarity to leave comfort zones. Moses had just died. The Israelites were stuck with a desert behind them and a wall in front of them when an unproven leader Joshua speaks a Word from the Lord: "Consecrate yourselves, for tomorrow the Lord is going to do amazing things in your life" (Joshua 3:1-5).

Too often, we become self-reliant. Self-absorbed in doing things our way. We are stuck in our traditions—how our parents did things. We don't know any other way to be a spouse or parent, because we never asked for one. We don't have a new business strategy because we have never prayed for a new model. We don't grow because we are content where we are. But God wants to do amazing things in our future—something He has never done before. He wants to take you where you have never dreamed or imagined. You don't know how to accomplish this task alone. You cannot take this city by yourself. *So don't!*

When you are preparing to face giants—stronger and mightier than you—don't make up your own way. Don't trust you—trust God. You've never been here before. Ask God for His plan—His blueprint. We haven't lived long enough to figure it out ourselves. We must gain new perspectives. There must be continuous improvement of processes—of how we do things. The moment we get complacent, stop learning, and stop exercising our faith, we degenerate—we stop growing from that point.

God places mentors, coaches, and pastors in our life to maximize us. Martin Henderson, who wrote headlines for the Los Angeles Times, mentored me to be a sports journalist at OC Sidelines when my sons were in high school. Martin was honored as the National Headline Writer of the Year for 2018 in Market/Industry/PR by American Copy Editors Society (ACES). He was extremely tough on me. I owe him a great deal for pouring his years of experience in me to get me to this place.

On numerous occasions, my writing mentor, Leslie Stobbe, shared sharp constructive criticism while I completed this book. He was somewhat taken aback at how I embraced his critique. But this book was eighteen years in the making. I needed mentors, like Martin, Les, Susan Stewart, and Christen Jeschke to help it come to reality. I needed to soak up all of their wisdom—to learn how to communicate this message to you. They were the "Aarons" God sent into my life for such a time as this.

Joshua told the Israelites, "The Presence of God is getting ready to move. When you see it, move! Get behind Him. Something greater is before us. Don't stay here. Don't make excuses. Pack your bags. Fulfill your dreams. Do wonders. March on what you want—conquer new territory. Slay your giants. Don't do business, church, or relationships as usual. Don't do you. Your ancestors kept you in one place for forty years with no change in position. It's time to go. To fulfill what He promised. He will not fail you. He will do extraordinary things in your life." (Joshua 3:5, 9-13, author's paraphrase)

When facing an unconquered giant, we will be filled with excuses. We will be tempted to lie about habits in order to keep them alive. We must realize that no one is going to kick us out of bed to pray. Read. Write chapters. Exercise, or work on our dream. No one is going to take our temptations away. We must flee them. We must completely sever old patterns, rituals, and thought patterns that can grow into generational giants. Satan wants to exterminate every trace of our influence. Because the Father of Lies will always try to compromise the Father of Faith. To choose Hagar instead of Sarah. To make Ishmael instead of Isaac. When we try to change our life, he will try to get us to resurrect old rituals. Our eyes on the wrong things— watching or listening to things God hates. Our thoughts on the wrong people—resurrecting old resentments and patterns. Sometimes, things may get worse before they get better. But change is coming. God is marching before, besides, and behind us. Stay steady. Leave everything that trapped you in the wilderness behind. This is not the season to be the same or be at ease.

So don't.

CHAPTER 14

AN UNCONVENTIONAL GENERATION

God used a giant to make David a king. Too often, we wait for giants to arise before we fight them. But in his generation, King David lived in preparation for—not in response to—giants. He fought differently. He faced a Goliath when no one else would.

No matter who and where you are, there will be giants. Giants to intimidate you. Giants to trample your efforts. Giants to make you feel small. Insignificant. Inexperienced. Powerless—like there is nothing you can do about what they are saying. But as giant killers, we are fearless, bold, and unconventional. We don't fight with human reasoning. Human arguments. Human fear or anger. We fight with God's wisdom. With skills and weapons proved by faithfulness.

Goliath was a renowned and dangerous warrior—unlike any giant the Israelites had ever seen before. Saul and his men shook as he spoke (1 Samuel 17). No one moved. No one dared to challenge him. Because giants can not only cause you to be shaken, but also paralyzed with fear. Giants can silence your voice. They will mock you for showing up for battle. When a giant shook an entire nation, there was a giant killer named David who was unfazed by what he heard.

He wanted to fight him.

Why would King Saul put the fate of his entire kingdom into the hands of an inexperienced boy against a champion? Simple. David was all he had. No one else stood up to the challenge.

David's Weapons

How did David win? What made him different than the others?

1. David didn't know his own size.

Goliath said, "Send me a man to fight." Instead, Saul sent a boy. When David was anointed king, the Lord said to Samuel, "Do not look on his appearance" (1 Samuel 16:7).

As giant-killers, we cannot be despondent—moved by the appearance of things. Giants don't move God. Never surrender your dream—marriage, family, degree, job, home, or business—because the opposition is bigger. David didn't pay attention to the size of his giant. He knew the size of his God.

2. David was opportunistic.

He was a man after God's own heart. He took on tasks and projects no one wanted—that seemed impossible. In

1 Samuel 17:22-26, David wanted to know what the reward was for defeating Goliath. He had just been anointed future king by God. Now, in the next chapter of his life, he is looking for an opportunity to realize his dream and call to be king.

In ancient times, the heir apparent was the oldest son upon the father's death. That right belonged to Jonathan, David's friend. David wasn't in Saul's lineage to be king. He was proof that God can make you a king no matter who your father was. He can make you a queen, no matter who your mother was. David's gift made room for him—made him royalty. His anointing gave him a job or position he was unqualified for.

When we become a giant killer, God will give us a platform—a position we are not qualified for. Jonathan was next in line. But like David's seven brothers, God skipped over Jonathan and made him sacrifice his life for David's greater anointing. He made him love David as his own life—to give up his right to the throne promised to David—so there would be no conflict after Saul died (1 Samuel 16:17-18).

David rose to the challenge of Goliath with an opportunity to do something historic and impossible. He was ready to seize the chance his brothers were afraid to take. His family was dressed for war, but not fighting. They were shaken by what they saw. Terrified to try or fail—waiting for a spoon-fed victory. But not David. He was a warrior. He didn't back down from a fight. He seized opportunities no one believed he could win. When no one else would fight Goliath, David brought two sticks and five stones to the party. He developed his skill as a slinger when no one was looking. He had a devastating, unconventional weapon previously used to kill a lion and a bear.

3. David was bold and unconventional.

David was a slinger. In Judges 20:16, the seven hundred select left-handed troops show how lethal skilled slingers could be ("could sling a stone "at a hair and not miss.") So, while David faced a big giant, Goliath faced a bigger problem. He faced an opponent he was completely unprepared for. They tried to give David Saul's weapons, but he took them off. David had his own. He was a bold trash-talker, but his boast was in God.

In 1 Samuel 17:45-51, David told Goliath:

You come to me with sword, spear, and javelin, but I come to you in the name of the Lord of Heaven's Armies—the God of the armies of Israel, whom you have defied. Today the Lord will conquer you, and I will kill you and cut off your head. And then I will give the dead bodies of your men to the birds and wild animals, and the whole world will know that there is a God in Israel! And everyone assembled here will know that the Lord rescues his people, but not with sword and spear. This is the Lord's battle, and he will give you to us!" As Goliath moved closer to attack, David *quickly ran* out to meet him. Reaching into his shepherd's bag and taking out a stone, he hurled it with his sling and hit the Philistine in the forehead. The stone sank in, and Goliath stumbled and fell face down on the ground. So David triumphed over the Philistine with only a sling and a stone, for he had no sword. Then David ran over and pulled Goliath's sword from its sheath. David used it to kill him and cut off his head. (NLT, emphasis added)

When facing a giant, you must do what you say quickly, before someone talks you out of it. David ran to his obstacle and triumphed. Then he cut off the head of Goliath with his own sword. He was fast, fearless, but also prepared. Likewise, what we have worked on—when no one was looking, when there was no recognition, when no one said thank you or patted us on the back—is preparing to feed us in the face of opposition.

Watch David's post-victory demeanor in 1 Samuel 17:53-57:

Then the Israelite army returned and plundered the deserted Philistine camp. (David took the Philistine's head to Jerusalem, but he stored the man's armor in his own tent). As Saul watched David go out to fight the Philistine, he asked Abner, the commander of his army, "Abner, whose son is this young man?" "I really don't know," Abner declared. "Well, find out who he is!" the king told him. As soon as David returned from

killing Goliath, Abner brought him to Saul with
the Philistine's head still in his hand. (NLT)

Now when you come into the presence of a king, you
come clean, shaven, and anointed with fragrant oil. But
when David comes into the presence of King Saul, his
adrenaline is flowing so much, he still has the head of
Goliath in his hand. This was the biggest victory of his
life. He wasn't supposed to win. Everyone knew it. But he
comes into the presence of the king, holding the head of
the giant who melted Saul and his army's hearts with fear.
As a giant killer, God will give you the answer to your
family or city's biggest problem.

What was the difference between the giant David saw,
and the giants the ten Israelite spies saw? The ten lived
in worry. David lived constantly in worship. The ten were
afraid. David had faith. The Israelites were spies. David
was a giant killer.

4. David was a problem solver.

To fulfill a dream, you must solve a problem. You must
be an answer or solution to someone.

David was Saul's answer to Goliath. David didn't have
to stage a coup, assassinate Saul, or divide the kingdom to
become king. David's gift kept him close to the throne. He
had plenty of opportunities to become king more quickly.
In 1 Samuel 26, Saul was asleep right in front of David.
But he would not take the throne by killing the previously
anointed king. He would wait. David told Abishai: "Don't

kill him. For who can remain innocent after attacking the LORD's anointed one? Surely the LORD will strike Saul down someday, or he will die of old age or in battle. The LORD forbid that I should kill the one he has anointed!" (v.9-11 NLT).

There was a season when David was a giant killer and a season when he was a cave dweller. In both, he was still a king. David trusted God's timing for him. Saul was God's problem, *not his*. Be patient. God will give you the throne and position you have dreamed about. In the waiting seasons of your life, surround yourself with mighty men and women. Commit to getting stronger and not weaker (2 Samuel 3). Be unconventional. Be mighty in your generation.

What we do for others is never lost or wasted.

Moses's Weapons

God could have wiped Pharaoh and Egypt's slave masters out in one day (Exodus 9:13-16). But He kept Pharaoh alive and hardened his heart, to demonstrate His power. To make Himself known in all the earth. To instill the fear of His people into the hearts of giants holding their dreams hostage in Jericho (fulfilled in Joshua 2:10-11). He gave the Israelites seven obstacles—seven giants—so they could show their children how to over-come them in life.

Giants are raised up, so the world can see Jesus at work in us. Exodus 10:1-3 records, "Then the LORD said to Moses, "Go to Pharaoh, for I have hardened his heart and the hearts of his officials so that I may perform these signs of mine among them that you may tell your children and grandchildren how I dealt harshly with the Egyptians and how I performed my signs among them, and that you may know that I am the LORD" (NIV).

Everything God did through the Israelites was for future generations. The next generation is not just our descendants. They are our legacy. As future ancestors, our responsibility is profound. Stay alive to tell your story. Generations are counting on you to tell how you crushed and overcame obstacles.

Our Weapons

In Exodus 1:8-10, we see how a lesser in number oppressor can subdue a greater in number people with cruel, bitter treatment, and systemic brainwashing.

That's what happened in Jonestown.

Even though the victims were greater in number than Jim Jones—their oppressor—they never mobilized to attack him or his henchmen. There was distrust. No one heard their silent screams of resistance.

Some of us are like that—living with a mindset where we accept whatever condition or fate our life, marriage, relationships, careers, or dreams are in. We accept abuse. Mistreatment. Narcissistic giants shouting down our voices, dreams, and opinions.

But today is the day we silence that giant.

Declare today: I will not give my freedom of speech or choice away. I will not submit my mind to relationships that suppress it. I will not transmit unaddressed fears, habits, or traumas to people—or let hostility triumph over healing.

Generations are watching how we evolve and grow.

When we kill our giants (fear, dissatisfaction, pride, addiction, laziness, procrastination, folly, bad family history, etc.), we teach the next generation how to silence theirs.

EPILOGUE

FINAL WORD

"If a prophet, or one who foretells by dreams, appears among you and announces to you a sign or wonder, and if the sign or wonder spoken of takes place, and the prophet says, 'Let us follow other gods (gods you have not known) and let us worship them,' you must not listen to the words of that prophet or dreamer. The LORD your God is testing you to find out whether you love him with all your heart and with all your soul" (Deut. 13:1-4 NIV).

In Jonestown, the people failed the biggest test of their lives.

Jim Jones was a false prophet. He created false signs and wonders. He led his members away from, instead of towards God. The people fell in love with a man instead of Jesus.

When the test of your love comes, will you be ready? Will you keep people in your life who love the Lord, with all their heart and soul, more than they love you? Will you love your Maker more than material things?

Jonestown proved that people can become deadly idols in our lives. We can allow the impact of people's decisions to become a throne where we constantly worship. An idol can be a person, lifestyle, job, ministry, religion, political party, habit, or addiction that takes first place in our life (not just a golden statue).

In Genesis 22, God wanted to know if Abraham loved Him more than what he had only "one" of in his life (a biological son). In verses 1-3, the Bible records:

Sometime later God tested Abraham. He said to him, "Abraham!" "Here I am," he replied. Then God said, "Take your son, your only son, whom you love—Isaac—and go to the region of Moriah. Sacrifice him there as a burnt offering on a mountain I will show you." (NIV)

Later in verse 12, God said, "Do not lay a hand on the boy. Do not do anything to him. Now I know that you fear God, because you have not withheld from me your son, your only son" (NIV).

God always wants what we love the most.

It is no coincidence that King David, one of the greatest giant killers in the Bible, was a lover of God, worship, truth, and justice more than anything else. But David was not perfect. He was just healed and forgiven.

We can be too.

The human body was created to heal in rehabilitation, not dwell in it. We are supposed to go through therapy, not live stuck in it. How many years have you been imprisoned by what broke your heart?

Wouldn't it be great if a broken heart could heal as fast as a broken bone? Why does it take longer? Our heart is filled with memories, both healed and fractured. Bodies heal. Memories last forever. But God can erase the shame of our past from memory.

Isaiah wrote this: "Don't be afraid—you're not going to be embarrassed. Don't hold back—you're not going to come up short. You'll forget all about the humiliations of your youth, and the indignities of being a widow will fade from memory" (Isa. 54:4 MSG).

Shame is a giant, not a resident in your life. We don't have to let bad memories master us with a death sentence.

In Chapter 5, I referenced Isaiah 26:13-14: "O Lord, our God, other masters besides You have ruled over us, but we will acknowledge and mention Your name only. They [the former tyrant masters] are dead, they shall not live and reappear; they are powerless ghosts, they shall not rise and come back. Therefore, You have visited and made an end of them and caused every memory of them [every trace of their supremacy] to perish" (AMP).

There are some masters in our lives we have submitted to that Jesus wants to end.

He came to destroy our giants and put an end to everything oppressive. Everything binding, unlawful, and tormenting. To make them a powerless ghost or memory in our life. To wipe out every trace of sin's dominance, supremacy, and shame in our lives.

He says,

"The giants in our rear-view mirror are
Former, but I am now.
Past, but I am present.
Old, but I make all things new.
Shameful, but I restore honor.

I am strength when they make you feel weak.
I am life when they condemn you.
I am shelter when you feel unsafe.

Your giants will not live and reappear repeatedly in
your life.
They will not rise and continue to haunt you from
the dead.
You will not acknowledge or mention them anymore.
You will not talk about them.
You will only talk about what I have done in your life."

That's what Jesus does.

He heals the scrapes and bruises in our lives. He erases the errors we have made, so we can write new chapters in life—a bestseller that transforms generations.

However, it is good to remember some things. There are memorials that remember the victims of the Holocaust and 9/11. We celebrate their lives with poems and inscriptions that say, "We remember..." They are poignant reminders so that we will never forget our history and the victims will not have died in vain.

In the Jonestown pavilion over the dead bodies, a sign hung with a quote from George Santayana that read: *"Those that do not remember the past are condemned to repeat it."*

It serves as a lesson to us today.

Don't forget the decisions that shaped, impacted, and scarred your family history up to this point. Remember the transitional places in your life. Remember how God took you from your worst season to your best season. From a bad place to a better place. Don't forget the stone that crushed the head of your Goliath.

The stones are truths and reminders to future generations of where God brought us from. Our children and those we lead are designed for increase. We must enlarge them to do more than us. Holding nothing back, we must drive our stakes into the ground and make additions to the places we are building. We must arm them to revitalize the places we have neglected—to kill the giants we let live.

Someone once said, "A tree is best measured lying down." You learn something new about yourself when you are knocked down. Dreams come to pass in the worst of circumstances. The most creative "you" is often birthed out of crisis.

My wife once said, "God works greatness out of our deepest suffering."

Arise giant killer, arise. Your greatness is coming.

REFERENCES

Prologue

1. Andy Kopsa, "The U.S. Military Had to Clean Up After the Jonestown Massacre 40 Years Ago. What the Crew Found Was 'Beyond Imagination," (*Time. com*, November 16, 2018). https://time.com/longform/jonestown-aftermath/
2. "Jonestown: The Life and Death of People's Temple," PBS, *American Experience* features. https://www.pbs.org/wgbh/americanexperience/features/jonestown-bio-leo-ryan/
3. FBI Records: The Vault, *Jonestown* 2:7-8, FBI FOIA. https://vault.fbi.gov/jonestown
4. FBI Records: The Vault, *Jonestown* 1: 64, FBI FOIA. https://vault.fbi.gov/jonestown

Chapter 1

1. "rescue," dictionary.com. 2019. https://www.dictionary.com/browse/rescue?s=t

Chapter 2

1. "Seven Types of Spirits," http://shamah-elim.info/girgash.htm, (May 2004).
2. Chicago UPI, "Hundreds Were Slain, Survivor Reportedly Says," FBI Vault (*Los Angeles Times* Nov 25, 1978), 104. https://vault.fbi.gov/jonestown/jonestown-part-280-of

Chapter 3

1. "The Hittites," http://shamah-elim.info/hittite.htm, (June 19, 2004).
2. Marshall Kilduff and Phil Tracy, "Inside People's Temple," (*New West Magazine*, August 1, 1977), 34.

Chapter 4

1. "The Girgashites," http://shamah-elim.info/girgash.htm, (May 2004).
2. Jacob Neighbors, "Obey Your Father, Jim Jones Rhetoric of Deadly Persuasion," para. 18-19. (*Alternative Considerations of Jonestown and Peoples Temple*). https://jonestown.sdsu.edu/?page_id=34307
3. Stephen Diamond, PhD, "Anger Disorder (Part Two): Can Bitterness Become a Mental Disorder?", para 1-2, (*Psychology Today*, June 3, 2009). https://www.psychologytoday.com/us/blog/evil-deeds/200906/anger-disorder-part-two-can-bitterness-become-mental-disorder

Chapter 5

1. "The Amorites," shamah-elim.info http://shamah-elim.info/amorite.htm, (June 12, 2004).
2. "distress," *KJV Dictionary* (2019). https://av1611.com/kjbp/kjv-dictionary/distress.html
3. Kenny Bryant, quoted in a personal session at National Institute of Marriage.
4. "diothosis," BibleGatway.com: *The Passion Translation Commentary* (2019). https://www.biblegateway.com/passage/?search=Hebrews%209:9-11&version=TPT
5. Charles Spurgeon, "Truth Stranger Than Fiction, Delivered on the Lord's Evening, May 30, 1886," para 1-2, (Christian Classics Ethereal Library). https://www.ccel.org/ccel/spurgeon/sermons35.xx.html

Chapter 6

1. "The Canaanites," http://shamah-elim.info/cananite.htm, (July 17, 2004).
2. Tracy, N., "Types of Addiction: List of Addictions," para. 4 and 6, (*HealthyPlace*, January 12, 2012. Retrieved on August 3, 2020). https://www.healthyplace.com/addictions/addictions-information/types-of-addiction-list-of-addictions
3. "Goliath," (*behindthename.com* 2020). https://www.behindthename.com/name/goliath

4. Matthew Henry, *Concise Commentary on the Whole Bible* (Bible Gateway). https://www.biblegateway.com/resources/matthew-henry/Job.31.1-Job.31.8

5. Kelly McGonigal, *The Willpower Instinct: How Self-Control Works, Why it Matters, and What You Can Do to Get More of It,* (Avery; reprint edition, December 31, 2013).

6. Milan and Kay Yerkovich, *How We Love*, (Waterbrook, Crown Publishing Group, A Division of Penguin Random House, LLC, New York, 2017).

7. Max DePree, *Treasure Quotes.* https://www.treasurequotes.com/quotes/we-cannot-become-what-we-want-by-remaining-wha

8. "dissolution," *Webster's Revised Unabridged Dictionary.* https://www.websters1913.com/words/Dissolution

9. "dissolution," *Strong's Exhaustive Concordance*, 2646, (*Bible Hub*). https://biblehub.com/strongs/greek/2646.htm

10. "plain," *Strong's Exhaustive Concordance*, 3769, (*Bible Hub*). https://biblehub.com/hebrew/3769.htm

11. Brene Brown, *"You Can Choose Courage or You Can Choose Comfort. But You Cannot Have Both,"* Quote *Notebook Journal* (Empowerment, June 17, 2019).

Chapter 7

1. "The Perizzites," http://shamah-elim.info/perizite.htm, (July 3, 2004).

2. *Wickline v. State of California* (1986) - 192 Cal. App. 3d 1630, 239 Cal. Rptr. 810.

3. "Perizzite," *King James Bible Dictionary* 2020. http://kingjamesbibledictionary.com/Dictionary/Perizzite

4. "village," *Webster's 1828 Dictionary, New James Bible Dictionary* 2020. http://kingjamesbibledictionary.com/Dictionary/village

5. Oscar Wright, quoted speaking at the Jonestown Memorial Services

6. Richard Avramenko, *Courage: The Politics of Life and Limb,* (University of Notre Dame Press, October 30, 2011).

Chapter 8

1. "The Hivites," http://shamah-elim.info/hivite.htm, (July 10, 2004).

Chapter 9

1. "The Jebusites," http://shamah-elim.info/jebusite.htm, (June 5, 2004).

2. "folly," *The Free Dictionary* 2020. https://www.thefreedictionary.com/folly

3. Ken Sande, *Peacemaking for Families* (Focus on the Family, 2002).

Chapter 10

1. *Holy Bible*, New International Version, Deuteronomy 20:16 Footnote ®, NIV® Copyright © 1973, 1978, 1984, 2011 by Biblica, Inc.® Used by permission. All rights reserved worldwide.

2. "Family History is Important to Your Health," *Understanding Genetics: A New York, Mid-Atlantic Guide for Patients and Health Professionals*-Appendix B, (National Library of Medicine, Washington, DC, Genetic Alliance, Jul 8, 2009). https://www.ncbi.nlm.nih.gov/books/NBK115560/

3. John Judge, "But Just Suppose It Didn't Happen That Way," para. 6-8, *The Black Hole of Guyana: The Untold Story of the Jonestown Massacre*, (*ratical.org*, 1985). http://www.ratical.org/ratville/JFK/JohnJudge/Jonestown.html

4. Caitlin Gibson, "40 years ago, this journalist survived the Jonestown massacre. He warns it could happen again," para. 10, (*Washington Post*, November 18, 2018). https://www.washingtonpost.com/lifestyle/style/40-years-ago-this-journalist-survived-the-jonestown-massacre-he-warns-it-could-happen-again/2018/11/16/bae22596-e9aa-11e8-b8dc-66cca409c180_story.html

Chapter 12

1. "Accusation of Human Rights Violations by Rev. James Warren Jones Against Our Children and Relatives at the Peoples Temple Jungle Encampment in Guyana, South America," (April 11, 1978).
2. "Truth and Lies: Jonestown, Paradise Lost," *ABC 20/20*, (produced by Muriel Pearson, aired Sept. 28, 2018).
3. The Jonestown Institute, Q134 Transcript (para 7). https://jonestown.sdsu.edu/?page_id=27339
4. Charles A. Krause, "Cult Leader Earmarked $7 Million for Soviets," para 1, (*The Washington Post*, December 18, 1978). https://www.washingtonpost.com/archive/politics/1978/12/18/cult-leader-earmarked-7-million-for-soviets/87cff75b-5dfe-4d7b-952f-008b7c-c88e2e/

Chapter 13

1. Gene Edwards, *A Tale of Three Kings: A Study in Brokenness*, (Tyndale House Publishers, 1992).

Bible References

NLT

Holy Bible, New Living Translation, copyright © 1996, 2004, 2015 by Tyndale House Foundation. Used by permission of Tyndale House Publishers, Inc., Carol Stream, Illinois 60188, USA. All rights reserved.

AMP

All rights reserved. For Permission To Quote information visit http://www.lockman.org/

NIV

Scripture quotations taken from *The Holy Bible*, New International Version® NIV®. Copyright © 1973, 1978, 1984, 2011 by Biblica, Inc.® Used by permission. All rights reserved worldwide. The "NIV" and "New International Version" are trademarks registered in the United States Patent and Trademark Office by Biblica, Inc.™

MSG

Scripture quotations marked MSG are taken from *THE MESSAGE*, copyright © 1993, 2002, 2018 by Eugene H. Peterson. Used by permission of NavPress. All rights reserved. Represented by Tyndale House Publishers, Inc.